LOWLAND SCOTTISH VILLAGES

Lowland Scottish Villages

MAURICE LINDSAY

ROBERT HALE · LONDON

© *Maurice Lindsay 1980*
First published in Great Britain 1980

ISBN 0 7091 7469 1

Robert Hale Limited
Clerkenwell House
Clerkenwell Green
London EC1

PRINTED IN GREAT BRITAIN BY
CLARKE, DOBLE & BRENDON LTD.
PLYMOUTH AND LONDON

Contents

I wish to acknowledge the help of Miss Helen Logan in deciphering and typing from my manuscript; that of Mr R. D. Cramond for his kindness in proof reading; and that of my daughter, Mrs Seona Barr, for preparing the index.

Illustrations

I

Before Starting Out

WHAT is a village? What, indeed, is Lowland Scotland? To both these seemingly simple questions there could be widely differing answers.

Once, during the 1939–45 war, in a thoughtless midnight moment, I referred to the Burmese town of Myitkyina as "a city". The document in which this indiscretion occurred had a restricted but unusually distinguished readership, which included His Majesty King George VI and the chief of the Imperial Staff, Sir Alan Brooke, as he then was. Neither of these readers took exception to my description, but a third reader did: the Prime Minister of this island kingdom, a certain Mr Winston Churchill. Accordingly I, a very junior staff officer in the War Office, was summoned one morning after breakfast to the august presence to defend myself. "Are you the officer who described Myitkyina as a city?" I was asked through a cloud of cigar smoke. I confessed my crime. "Justify yourself," came the command.

Naturally, I was not so foolish as to appear before the most important person then living in Britain without having thought out some kind of defence. I therefore proceeded to reel off the best I could collect in the way of appropriate statistics; population figures, the number of pagodas and temples the place possessed, even the name of Myitkyina's cinema. My attempted justification of Myitkyina's elevation to major urban status, however, was of no avail. "But has it a *cathedral?*" the famous voice thundered,

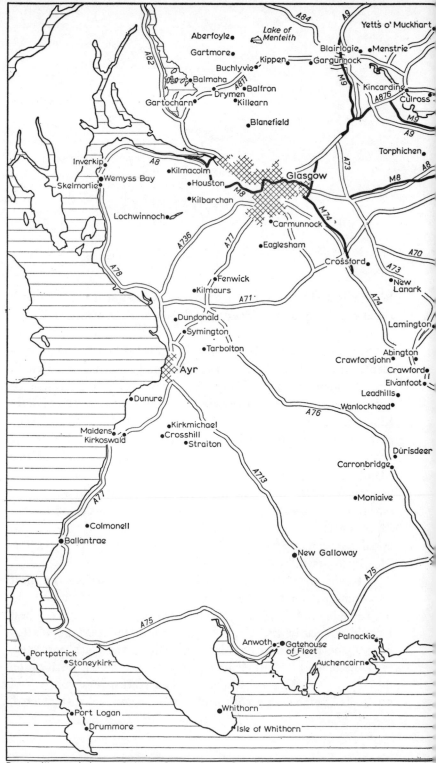

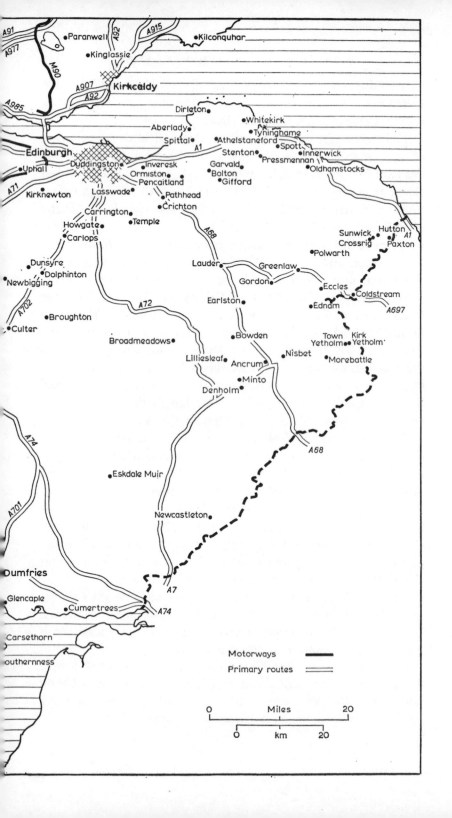

characteristically emphasizing the middle syllable. I admitted that it had not. "Then in future call it a township," he pronounced, dismissing me with a wave of his cigar.

While no reader of this book is likely to wield the same power of keeping an author on his toes as did Churchill all these years ago (which is just as well, because my toes are now a good deal less elastic than they were in the winter of 1944–45), a rough definition of both terms should at least avoid misunderstandings. Strictly speaking, all that is not Highland is Lowland. However, for the purposes of this book, my villages run south and east of the crofting counties, and so take in, albeit briefly, the flat coastal belt which runs up to Wick and Thurso, and to some extent shares a culture only partly Scottish with Orkney and Shetland. But they include none of the Hebridean islands; not the Lews, which reach up to steep rocky heights but have also much flat land, nor Tiree, which is as flat as most of the counties in Southern England. In other words, this book makes no forays into those parts of Scotland where traditionally, in however diluted a form, the culture of the Gael still holds sway. Indeed, Gaeldom is the province, in a companion volume, of my friend James Shaw Grant.

To define topographical limitations is one thing. To draw a dividing line between a large village and a small town is quite another. In New York, the name Greenwich Village denotes the familiar haunt of people with a common interest in the arts rather than an accurate topographical description. Much the same goes for those districts in London, long since incorporated into the Great Wen, but whose inhabitants feel so strong a consciousness of a surviving identity, and such an affection for their own locales that to them 'villages' they remain.

Technically speaking, a planner would probably regard a village as a place housing a maximum of three thousand inhabitants. Once the population grows beyond that figure, increased shopping or other facilities soon turn it into a town.

I give no promise that I have counted the number of people living in every place visited during this book's itinerary, if for no other reason than that one of the most serious problems affecting rural life—in Scotland, as elsewhere—has for years been the prob-

lem of the expanding village. Many an old-established village,
sleepily evolving at a slow enough rate throughout the nineteenth
and the first half of the twentieth centuries, has suddenly found
itself faced with the prospect of being girt about with council
housing schemes, radically altering its physical appearance and
sometimes also its sociological character.

A huge amount of damage was inflicted on the rural heritage
during the 'fifties. Many agricultural villages had their sturdy old
fabric condemned simply because cottages lacked such easily pro-
vidable facilities as damp courses, electricity and a mains water
supply. In such cases, the occupants were often moved into newly-
built and, at that time, usually ungainly standardized council
houses. The old cottages, if not speedily bulldozed into dusty rubble
for road-bottoming or building-site foundations, were sold to commuting city dwellers, who thereupon proceeded to modernize them.
In this way the character of many villages within easy travelling
distances of cities or larger towns was altered, even if the fabric
of the village core was saved. Villages with a commuting potential,
however, were often the lucky ones.

In those brave post-Second War days, when mandatory planning
first entered our lives, and the suddenly swollen ranks of ill-trained
mandatory planners uttered decrees in a manner more befitting
mandarins than servants of the people; when the supply of public
money was thought to be unlimited, and the old automatically
equitable with the bad (the concept of conservation being then
still two decades into the future); when the speed of physical change
was being increased to a pace which many people found psycho-
logically disturbing, greater havoc was wrought on the substance of
our heritage than our umquhile enemies had succeeded in inflicting
during the six years of war. Most of it was done in the name of
'progress', that most dangerous word used to justify almost anything
where quick profit or short-term political advantages are at stake.

Not long after I had moved into a cottage in the centre of a
'rescued' village from which the older agricultural population had
been moved, reluctantly, into new council houses that had recently
begun to hulk greyly upon its fringe, the young milkman rang the
bell to present his account.

"D'ye like livin in this auld hoose?" he mused disbelievingly, as I searched for money to pay him. "You've just newly come, aye? Well, if ye stay here lang enough, I daresay ye'll qualify fur one o' thae grand new cooncil hooses."

To be fair, the planner of today is a very different creature from his predecessor of the 'forties. For one thing, he is better trained and so likely to be much less arrogant. The considerable growth in the number of local Civic or Amenity Societies established throughout these islands is but one sign of an increasing public insistence by those who are planned-for that they must have some say in processes of decision-making which may affect them. No longer can a planner—or, for that matter, a planning committee—seek to impose from the remote security of some committee room an unpopular decision and expect to get away unchallenged. "Public participation in the Planning Process" has even been legally assured by 'seventies legislation.

In addition, conservation laws have now been greatly strengthened. Not many villages may possess more than a few individually listed buildings, group value being the substance of their attractiveness. However, the overall protection now accorded to conservation areas created by the Civic Amenities Act of 1967 and strengthened by the Town and Country Planning (Scotland) Act, 1974, is likely to benefit many Scottish villages that retain their character, whether they be Highland or Lowland. It must be hoped that soon the new awareness, which the evolution of our conservation laws has produced, may result in much greater care being taken where village expansion becomes necessary.

Villages, like towns and cities, are living, growing entities. They cannot simply be frozen into lifeless museum pieces. Hitherto, they have evolved slowly, to meet either long-continuing uses and needs, or to adapt to new ones, taking their gradual place in the economic pattern of rural life. The sudden leap of activity following 1946—partly a reaction against the static years of war, partly a misinterpreted response to the very real needs of the changing collective social conscience—often brought with it an urge to destroy what was mellow and traditional. New and insufficiently tried techniques were uniformly applied to aspects of living as different in their needs as building and education, with consequences a generation later far from happy. A dramatic increase in the number of car-owning families, and the switch from the railways to the roads of much industrial and commercial traffic, led to the demand for new and better roads, and the thoughtless and unimaginative destruction of old town centres, particularly in England, to provide space for them.

With the gradual abandonment of city and town centres as residential areas, private builders often coped with the demand for rural living equally as insensitively as the local authorities. All too often, private dwellings have been chosen out of a builder's catalogue containing houses sometimes not even through-designed by an architect in the first place, and marketed primarily to fill the average purchaser's dream-house expectation-gap rather than to fit sensitively into well-established surroundings.

Although hard economic times are always likely to evolve cost-factors stringent enough to make cheapness a prime consideration, the standard of house design has improved over the past three decades, especially in the local authority sector. But village expansion still needs careful treatment, stock suburban solutions being nearly always inappropriate.

New times, of course, produce new needs. No one would seriously suggest that twentieth-century men and women should have to accept nineteenth- or eighteenth-century standards of hygiene or comfort. Happily, the focus upon the limited supplies of many world resources, forced upon Western civilization by the Arab-Israeli war of 1973, makes rehabilitation and conservation for the first time seem to the young ethically, as well as economically and socially, a desirable aim. Modern conservation methods can meet both twentieth-century practical housing requirements as well as help preserve that sense of psychological continuity so essential to us in a ruthless, too-rapidly changing technological age.

The best of our heritage, whether urban or rural, also makes up an important part of the capital assets of our tourist industry. Tourists do not travel hundreds of increasingly expensive miles to examine our high-rise flats, erected regardless of the impact they make upon their surroundings; or to browse amongst the geometri-

cal monotonies of council or private housing estates. They come to
experience and, it may be hoped, to enjoy the grandeur of our
Georgian and Victorian cityscapes; our cathedrals and our castles
and the grand houses of the rich and famous in past ages. But they
also come to savour the peace of our villages, made up of little
houses built through the centuries to traditional patterns for generations of ordinary folk.

It is amongst such little houses and cottages, grouped into villages
or hamlets throughout the Scottish Lowlands, that we shall browse
in the following pages. Needless to say, not every village can be
mentioned, or, indeed, would necessarily be worthy of notice, not
having the charm of setting, the quality of fabric, or the colouring
of human history to provide distinction. The aim of what follows
is, therefore, to try to enhance the enjoyment of the traveller who
finds himself resting in, or exploring, what seem to me to be the
more interesting of Scotland's Lowland villages.

The reorganization of local government in Scotland during the
summer of 1975 left many Scots with the wish to see it reorgan-
ized yet again, at least in part along more locally sensitive lines.
I have therefore decided not to use the new divisions and nomen-
clature of the regions or districts, preferring instead the postal
counties grouped under airts or directions which seem to acknowledge generally recognized affinitive qualities. My groupings thus
are: The Borderlands; the Lothians; West and South-West; Fife
and Kinross; the Heart of Scotland; East and North-East; and the
Far North.

Finally, I should like to stress that a book which singles out
villages, together with some of the more important castles or houses
that may once have affected their growth or development, is necessarily indulging in the over-focusing of a kind of selective detail
that makes the depiction of encompassing historical, sociological
and linguistic considerations necessarily impossible. I therefore
stress again that this book is intended primarily as a travelling
companion for all who have a special interest in the domestic
images of Lowland Scottish life as they are reflected in villages,
and is no sense intended to be a substitute for general or more
detailed works of reference.

2

The Borderlands

VILLAGES gather themselves together for varying reasons, usually economic. While many ancient burghs developed out of a cluster of houses, or villages, built around a castle to meet the needs of its inhabitants—Castle Fraser, in Aberdeenshire, still has its own 'village' attached to the main structure—rural villages directly supporting neither castle nor ecclesiastical establishment brought together the men who tended the land, and those who provided and sold such services and other necessities of life that were not simply a by-product of daily effort in the fields. In the Border country there was another cogent reason for cottages to group together, apart from the normal human instinct of gregariousness: defence against threatening forces from outside. Doubtless the feeling of security produced by collectivity was largely illusory, for the threat to Border life, long after wolves had disappeared from Southern Scotland, came from English raiding-parties, and in some cases English armies. Against such forces intent on looting and burning, there can have been little enough defence. So there are no villages in Southern Scotland the fabric of which is of great antiquity.

Indeed, until comparatively modern times, the homes of ordinary Scots were built of wattle and clay. Froissart, who sojourned in Scotland in 1383 while French troops under Sir John de Vienne were doing their best to assist Robert III in his struggle against the English, recorded that because their homes were so frequently destroyed by the enemy, the houses of the Scots were constructed basically of six posts and some branches so that they could be rebuilt in two or three days. Old Roxburgh, an important town by medieval standards though probably not much more than a large village by the standards of today, has disappeared altogether, except for a vault beneath a rickle of stones where once its much-beleaguered fortalice stood. There is a village of later date, New Roxburgh, on the left bank of the Teviot, on a peninsula between Teviot and Tweed.

History faithfully records the doings of kings and generals, of negotiations and battles, of victories and defeats: but of the fate of the ordinary people profoundly affected by the wise or foolish actions of the great ones, it says scarcely a word. Yet the leaders could not accomplish their manœuvrings on their own:

> History says: this or that king built
> so many castles, had countless battle-scars,
> honour and guilt inextricably mixed
> Who laid the stones, put death into his wars?*

Alexander II was married in Roxburgh Castle, and great, no doubt, would be the nuptial celebrations among the villagers; celebrations repeated when, two years later, Alexander III was born there. During the next century, Roxburgh and its castle changed hands several times, until Edward Balliol surrendered it, along with the independence of Scotland, to Edward III in 1332. Various attempts by the Scots to regain the place by force failed, until on 3 August 1460, James II laid waste the houses and besieged the castle, employing a cannon nicknamed 'The Lion' because of its powerful calibre. Standing too close to it, the king was killed when it blew up. His queen hurried to the site with her eight-year-old son, and so inspired the troops that the English were driven out of a stronghold they had held for many decades, a victory that can have been of little consolation to the inhabitants of the shattered town, then the fourth largest in Scotland. To avoid any repetition of English occupancy, the victors razed the castle to the ground, although that fierce ravager of the Borders, Protector Somerset, had it partially rebuilt in 1547.

* "Responsibilities" from *Comings and Goings*, Akros Publications, 1971.

Today, if Roxburgh has a claim to distinction, it is because in the graveyard of its church lies the bluecoat beggar Andrew Gemmell—the blue coat was a kind of 'uniform' at a time when begging was regarded in the Lowlands as a more or less legitimate occupation—the prototype of Scott's Edie Ochiltree, in *The Antiquary*. Gemmell was so successful at his craft that he lived to lament the effects of inflation which, he claimed in his old age, had reduced his 'earning' capacity by some forty pounds a year.

I began this journey with Roxburgh, though today it is by no means a 'front-line' village, simply because it had royal connections, and at one time an ancestry far outgrowing village status.

But I could as well have begun with the village of Mordington, whose church door almost opens onto the highway from England. It has been united as a parish to Foulden, a conservation area village with a preserved harmony of detail about the cottage row containing the former smithy and school, and the grouping of the 1786 church, manse and the unique tithe barn. Lamberton, since 1650 also in the same parish, has an old tollhouse on the Border, and was once the scene of runaway marriage dramas similar to those that enlivened the more celebrated Gretna, at the western end of the borderline.

Some of the villages which lie near the eastern end of the Border are commemorated in one of those rhymes devised by anonymous poetasters living, presumably, in a place not amongst those named:

> Hutton for auld wives,
> Broadmeadows for swine,
> Paxton for drunken wives
> And salmon sae fine.
> Crossrig for lint and woo'
> Spittal for kale,
> Sunwick for cakes and cheese
> And lasses for sale.

Hutton, a little to the south of Whiteadder Water, has other claims to fame, apart from its female senior citizens. Edward I is supposed to have camped there in 1296, on the eve of the capture of Berwick—by the fortunes of war, an English town, but by geographical location and the dictates of common sense the obvious centre for the county of Berwickshire, although such arguments have never prevailed sufficiently with the English to persuade them to return what is *Scotia irredenta*—and the birthplace of Andrew Foreman, Archbishop of St Andrews from 1514 to 1522.

Its main claim to more recent fame is that the ugly Victorian mansion of Hutton House, adjacent to the ancient peel tower of Hutton Hall, became the last home of the shipowner Sir William Burrell (1861–1958), whose vast collection of pictures and *objets d'art*, one of the largest and most varied private collections ever assembled in Scotland, was bequeathed to Glasgow in 1944, which city, more than thirty-five years later, had failed to house it.† The castle itself, a monument to the futility of Victorian over-confidence, seems likely to subside into ruin. Hutton church, on the other hand, still survives, the third on the site, in 1835 re-placing the eighteenth-century edifice where local volunteers gathered, no doubt in fear and trembling, to await the threatened Napoleonic invasion of 1804.

Paxton, whatever the state of sobriety of its wives or the quality of its salmon from the Tweed, is said to be the place of origin of the tune for Lady Anne Barnard's song, "Robin Adair".

> Paxton's a fine snug place, Robin Adair,
> It's a wondrous couthie place Robin Adair,
> Let Whiteadder rin a spate,
> Or the wind blow at ony rate,
> Yet I'll meet thee on the gait, Robin Adair.

Paxton House, built towards the close of the eighteenth century by Robert Adam, has splendidly-fashioned plasterwork, and some remarkable overmantels and Regency furniture made for it by John Trotter of Edinburgh. When it was the home of George Home, one of the Edinburgh literati at the end of the eighteenth century and a member of the Mirror Club, it was visited by Henry Mac-kenzie, author of *The Man of Feeling*. Another visitor was the guardian of Burns's "Clarinda", Lord Craig.

---

† However, plans by Barry Gasson, the winner of a competition for the erection of a gallery in the grounds of Pollok House to house the Burrell Collection, have been agreed, and work commenced at a ceremony attended by the donor's daughter on 3 May 1978.

Ayton also has a castle, once the home of the Fordyce family, to give it a focal point, a work in red sandstone of James Gillespie Graham. A curious local legend insists that the building grew up without architect or plan. The original castle, Norman-built for the Baron de Vesci, was totally demolished by Surrey in 1498. The single street along which this village is laid, starts by the Water of Eye. It is crossed by a pleasant bridge. Near the present Victorian parish church, in First Pointed style, stand the humbler ruins of the pre-Reformation kirk, now gripped by ivy. Here, it is said, the representatives of the Scots and English kings met on more than one occasion to arrange truces, most of them, unfortunately, not kept for long. To the south-west of the church, the church lodge was formerly a tollhouse on the road from Berwick to Edinburgh.

The Eye follows a pastoral course to the fishing town of Eyemouth. On the coast the village of Burnmouth lies at the bottom of a gully, its one-time fishermen's cottages clinging to the foot of a steep rock-face.

Through Reston, built with the coming of the railway to be the junction for Coldingham, Grant's House, allegedly named after a cobbler who repaired the boots of the workmen employed on the construction of the Newcastle to Edinburgh line, and Cockburnspath, round the cliff-edged eastern fall of the Lammermuir Hills, the road to the North runs.

The village of Cockburnspath lies inland a little. It still possesses a mercat cross, reputedly dating from 1612, in the centre of a pleasant square. James VI and I created 'Co'path' (to give it its local pronunciation) a burgh of barony. On the south side of its original square there is a church dating in part from the fourteenth century, with a round tower, added in the late sixteenth or early seventeenth century, rising curiously out of the west gable. The group of buildings which lead from the square down to Cockburnspath Burn are also within the conservation area. They include the old manor-house, the mill and the smithy. A mile or so to the east of the village, on the edge of a ravine, stands Cockburnspath Tower, thought by some to be the prototype of Ravenswood Castle in Scott's novel *The Bride of Lammermoor*.

West of Pease Bay, popular with holidaymakers, the cliff-lined coast holds the hamlet of Cove, where a local laird, Sir John Hall, built a fishing harbour in 1831. Nothing brings more strongly home the traditionally localized nature of the Scottish fishing industry before the twentieth century than the presence of such wind-swept, spray-dashed clusters of cottages which are to be found at the foot of sea-cliffs right up the eastern seaboard of Scotland. St Abb's, on the coast between Eyemouth and Fast Castle—a gnarled, defiant stump, all that remains of this fortress where the Gowrie Plot to kidnap James VI is believed to have been hatched, and which later became Scott's Wolf's Crag in *The Bride of Lammermoor*—also has its cottaged streets winding down to a fishing harbour, in this case built in 1833 by a member of the brewing family of Usher. The picturesque rocky setting of St Abbs gives it a quality of its own.

The impact of repeated English invasions made a forceful impression on this eastern corner of Borderland. Coldingham, for instance, felt the violence of English arms when in 1314 King John set alight its priory, founded in 1068 by King Edgar of Scotland. Cromwell blasted it in 1648. What remains wears a fragmentary, slightly unconvincing look, doing service since 1854 as the parish church. A more recent restoration has improved the interior. The narrow winding streets of the old village give the place its intimate character, with the market cross at their centre.

Because Berwickshire was deprived of Berwick, its proper county town, when the skirmishing between the two nations cooled after 1603, Greenlaw shared the honour of serving as the former county's administrative centre from 1696 until 1853. Then Duns, unmistakably a town, took over half that honour, and gradually usurped its partner. Greenlaw, however, has remained a large linear village by the banks of the River Blackadder. The former County Buildings, the work of John Cunningham, put up in 1829, dominate the scene. They were converted into swimming baths in 1973. The old mercat cross of 1609 was pulled down and cast aside in 1829. Surprisingly, it turned up in 1887, minus its lion, lying in a basement of the church. It was then re-erected against the west wall of the church tower, once, in fact, a jail, though the courthouse which linked it with the church is no longer standing. The rows of comely houses around the area of the green, as well as those in East and West High Street, are all included in a conservation area.

Greenlaw, it seems also judged its girls by generalized rhyming, the verdict being:

> The lasses o' Lauder are mim and meek,
> The lasses o' the Fanns smell o' peat reek,
> The lasses o' Gordon canna sew a steek
> But weel can they sup their Crowdie!
> The lasses o' Earlston are bonnie and braw,
> The lasses o' Greenlaw are black as a craw,
> But the lasses o' Polwart are the best o' them a'

Of the places the qualities of whose womenfolk this rural connoisseur enumerated, Lauder is the most impressive. It sits in the middle of Lauderdale, originally closely connected with the home of the powerful Maitlands, latterly Earls of Lauderdale. Until the sixteenth century, their castle was known as Lauder Fort. But John, the first Duke of Lauderdale, employed Robert Mylne, Charles II's master mason, and the architect Sir William Bruce to reconstruct it into the present Thirlestane Castle. Bruce framed the narrow double-towered west elevation of the sixteenth-century castle by pavilion towers, and added an extra storey. A recessed entrance doorway was built at first-floor level, and the approach to the building was dignified and enhanced. The castle was further enlarged during the nineteenth century.

The Maitland family has contributed much to Scottish history. There was the famous, or infamous, 'chameleon', William Maitland of Lethington—Secretary Maitland, who was privy to the plans for the murders of both Rizzio and Darnley—and the building Duke of Lauderdale (1616–82), son of the second Lord Maitland. Lauderdale began life as a zealous Presbyterian and Covenanter, then veered round to Charles's cause. On Charles II's accession Lauderdale was made Secretary of State. He became an unbending Scottish administrator, opposed to the Covenanters. He received his dukedom in 1672, but died stripped of all his high offices. Another member of the family was the father of Secretary Maitland, Sir Richard Maitland (1496–1586), a lawyer who, on becoming blind at the age of sixty, turned poet, and left us some bitter comments on the manners of what he regarded as the new-fangled inflationary times:

> Now we have mair, it is weil kend,
> Nor our forebearis had to spend;
> Bot for less at the yearis end;
> And never has ane merry day;
> God will na riches to us send
> Swa lang as honour is away.

Lauder itself is today a pleasant village through which passes the A68 road. The eighteenth-century Tolbooth or Town Hall, dominates the town centre from its islanded position at the top of High Street. The other important public building is the old parish church of St Mary, also built by Sir William Bruce in 1673, though repaired in 1820 (when it was given a new pulpit), 1864 and 1973. Cruciform in plan, and with a 'loft' or gallery for the Lauderdale family as well as one for the burgh worthies, the crossing carries a central tower. It replaced the older church which stood, so to say, in the front garden of the castle when Bruce began his work of restoration.

Charming, too, is the Black Bull Hotel, put up, like most of Lauder, in the eighteenth century but added to in the nineteenth. Of the attractive houses, especially pleasing are No. 1 East High Street, and 20 and 22 Market Place. There is Cope's House, too, now a draper's shop, where the ill-fated Sir John Cope spent the night after his defeat at Prestonpans. The Smiddy also adds to the grouping of what has been designated as an outstanding conservation area, and one in which electricity lines were undergrounded as a contribution to European Architectural Heritage Year, 1975. Students of Scottish history will recall that it was from a no longer extant bridge just outside Lauder that Archibald 'Bell-the-Cat' Douglas played a leading role in hanging James III's hated favourites.

Of the other villages mentioned in the rhyme about female quality, Polwarth was the scene of annual merrymaking celebrated in a poem attributed to James I, "Polwart on the Green". One reason for the rhymester's assumption that the Polwarth lasses are "the best o' them a' " may be attributable to the presence of the Black Well, at the west end of the village. A stranger drinking its waters is said so to fall in love with the place that he will never be able to leave it.

Its parish church, the site of which has borne a place of worship since the tenth century, has a square bell-tower presented by the Marchmont family in 1703. It contains a bell curiously inscribed: "Given to the Kirk of Polwarth by Lady Grizel Kar, Countess of Marchmont, 1697. R. M. Fecit Edr. 1717." Somebody seems to have got their date wrong; unless, of course, it took a long time to cast.

One of the most romantic true stories in Border history centres on the vault at the east end of this church, where Sir Patrick Hume, later Earl of Marchmont, hid for a month from Charles II's soldiers until he was moved to a cellar in Redbraes to await escape to Holland. While at Polwarth, he was secretly fed by his courageous twelve-year-old daughter, Grizel, later to become the wife of George Baillie of Jerviswood. Grizel was also the author of a well-loved song, "O werena my hert licht I wad dee".

West Gordon gave its name to the Gordon tribe of gypsies. One of them, Jean Gordon, became the prototype of Scott's Meg Merrilees. The L-shaped ruined tower of Greenknowe, one-time residence of an ardent Covenanter, Willie Pringle, stands near the village.

Earlston was once known for more than girls who were "bonnie and braw". Because of its proximity to both the abbeys of Melrose and Dryburgh, it seems to have had some ecclesiastical importance, having been visited on several occasions by David I, that "sair sanct for the crown". The village certainly grew up around its medieval church. The present church dates from 1892, though the bell, from Middelburg in the Low Countries, was cast in 1609.

Earlston's other claim to fame is its alleged connection with True Thomas, Thomas of Ercildoune, or Thomas the Rhymer, our first half-identifiable Scots poet. But was he Sir Thomas Learmont of Ercildoune? Or Thomas Rimour? Did he really live in the ivy-clad tower bought in 1895 by the Edinburgh Borderers' Association as a memorial to the poet, but exposed by The National Trust for Scotland as being of much later construction than the thirteenth century? Did he actually write, or otherwise transmit, the great ballad that enshrines his shadowy name?

It is perhaps as well for modern Earlston that it is still in the harmless grip of poetic legend, for later physical developments have not been sympathetic to its romantic past.

Before we move south-west over to Roxburghshire, one other village that is a conservation area deserves a passing mention: Swinton, with its three-sided village green, in the middle of which is a classical column dated 1769. Its church of 1729 has a bell inscribed "Maria est nomen meum 1499". This neatly enclosed village, with its solid-looking houses facing against the carriageway, is built on a convexly-curving ridge. As a result, a walk down the main street gives one a feeling of being constantly surprised. The village has been extended by some visually unfortunate council housing.

Coldstream, Greenlaw, Gordon and Earlston look naturally to Kelso as their centre. So, too, do other nearby villages. St Boswells, at the junction of the Selkirk and Melrose roads, has a huge village green. This is fox-hunting country, and St Boswells is the home of the kennels of the Duke of Buccleuch's foxhounds. The Lauderdale and Jedforest packs also hunt this area of Scotland. St Boswells today is halfway between being a sizeable if scattered village and a small town, but retains a village green. Now, it is mainly a summer stopping-place for tourists. Once, however, every July, the green was the scene of one of southern Scotland's most imposing cattle and wool fairs, to which gypsies came as well as traders. Near St Boswells stands Lesudden House—Lesudden was the ancient name for the village—a charming late sixteenth-century home with a seventeenth-century wing built by the Scotts of Raeburn.

Ancrum, though nearer to Jedburgh than Kelso, is another village on the rim of the Kelso radial road system. It stands on a curve of the River Ale. It suffered at the hands of the Earl of Hertford in 1544, an experience avenged a year later when the Earl of Angus and Scott of Buccleuch routed an English force on Ancrum Moor, the two English leaders, Sir Ralph Evers and Sir

Bryan Latoun, being slain in the encounter. The village still possesses the shaft of its medieval mercat cross, said to date from the twelfth century.

Nisbet, a village on the right bank of the Teviot three miles east of Ancrum, was the birthplace of Samuel Rutherford, that fanciful, fiery preacher who became minister of Anwoth, in Galloway, and a leader of the forces supporting the National Covenant.

Moving further round the Kelso radial road-wheel, we come to Morebattle, a popular haunt of fishermen, who may be seen by the banks of the River Kale. Two nearby ruined towers, Corbet and Whitton, were both burnt by the English. Further round still lie Town Yetholm and Kirk Yetholm, two villages of peaceful beauty from which there is a splendid view across the English Cheviots.

The Yetholms were not always peaceful, however. It is said that a fifth of their inhabitants once earned their living smuggling Scotch whisky. Once, too, they celebrated the Fastern E'en games. Above all, the Yetholms were the home of the Border gypsies. The Faa family, being the gypsy 'Royal House', were the most famous. They maintained their own curious customs and titles. Exactly where they came from no one certainly knows, but they seem to have settled at Yetholm as long ago as the fifteenth century.

The most celebrated gypsy of them all was probably Jean Gordon, the prototype for Meg Merrilees. Scott met her granddaughter, Madge, a six-foot girl "dressed in a long red cloak, who commenced acquaintance by giving me an apple, but whom, nevertheless, I looked on with much awe". 'Meg Merrilees' Gordon married Patrick Faa and had four sons. Three of them, together with their wives, were hanged for sheep-stealing. The fourth was murdered by another gypsy. Patrick Faa was transported for fire-raising. Jean, a beggar in Carlisle in the aftermath of the rising of the 'Forty-five, publicly proclaimed her antipathy to the house of Hanover. For this, she was flung into the Eden and ducked again and again until left for dead. She managed to crawl to the bank, but was eventually found dead of exposure under a hedge.

Carham and Sprouston lie near the English frontier. Near Sprouston, the Scots routed three thousand English horsemen at Hadden Rigg during a skirmish in 1549. Birgham, which looks across the Tweed to English Carham, was a meeting-place for the making of treaties from 1018, when Malcolm II won the Lothians for the Scots. The most important of many such diplomatic meetings took place on 18 July 1290, when the signing of the Treaty of Birgham re-established Scotland's independence.

The attractive village of Ednam, on the banks of Eden Water, is famous because of Ednam Manse where, in 1700 James Thomson was born. He was brought up, however, at Southdean, to where his father soon moved. Thomson's greatest poem, "The Seasons", continued the nature tradition of the Scottish Makars. "Rule Britannia", part of a masque he provided for Dr Arne to set to music, established his wider British fame. Henry Francis Lyte, author of the once-popular hymn "Abide with me", was also born in Ednam.

Eccles, between the Rivers Leet and Tweed, has in its church-yard the ruins of a Cistercian nunnery, burnt down by Hertford. Near-by Kames was the birthplace of a judge of the Edinburgh eighteenth-century enlightenment, Henry Home, raised to the Bench in 1752 as Lord Kames, and the author of *Elements of Criticism*, amongst other books. On yet another of the radical roads, six miles from Kelso, is the village of Smailholm, dominated by Smailholm Tower, stark and ruined on Sandyknowe Crags. It exercised a powerful effect on the imagination of the young Walter Scott.

Perhaps the most charming of all the Border villages is Bowden, which combines both the characteristics of a linear village and that of a village with its own green. Its typical examples of Scottish domestic architecture, small in scale and predominantly of whin-stone and harl construction, are colour-washed with slate roofs, and form a close entity. The seemly way in which the buildings relate to each other, the spaces they create and the relationship with the rise or fall of the ground add much to its charm. The village church dates from the twelfth century, but was rebuilt in 1794. A further restoration occurred in 1909. During the eighteenth century, flax was grown in the surrounding crofts, and the weaving of linen became an important cottage industry. When the weavers moved into towns like Galashiels, agriculture reasserted itself as the village's main interest. Today, it is largely residential. The village cross is now situated on a grass bank outside Becketsfield House. The village fountain decorates the green, set against an attractive wicker gate in the stone wall of Bowden Knowe.

Hawick provides another centre from which to tour Border villages. Lilliesleaf, on the Ale Water, is one of the quietest. The font from the twelfth-century church is preserved in the present eighteenth-century church, altered in 1883 and added to in 1910. The Riddells of Riddell once occupied the 'big house', but they fell in a financial crash in 1819. Their great house was burnt down in 1943.

Beneath the Minto Hills lies the compact little village of Minto with its church, its manse, its 'big house' and row of once-attendant cottages. Minto House, the work of Archibald Elliot, was built for the first Earl of Minto, who took part in the impeachment of Warren Hastings. At the moment of writing it is still standing, but empty and, sadly, has been the subject of listed building consent for demolition. Minto Church was built to a Gothic design by Playfair in 1831. The original manse, built in imitation of a villa in Tuscany, was destroyed by fire in 1954. The deserted Fatlips Castle, once owned by the Turnbulls, stands to the east of the village, on the summit of Minto Crags.

The Tweedside village of Ladykirk has a delightful church built by James IV in gratitude after having nearly lost his life by drowning in the Tweed in 1499. It is thought to be one of the last churches built in Scotland before the Reformation. It now has a stone-slabbed roof, a defensive looking tower and a four-sided belfry added in 1743.

Denholm, in the parish of Cavers, has a rather English-looking village green associated with the stocking-weaving industry. It is a planned village dating mostly from the turn of the eighteenth to the nineteenth century. The Old Mill, at the rear of Greenview, has a series of small windows, each intended to light a stocking-machine. Westgate Hall is a good example of a seventeenth-century home. The church, with its clock tower and Italianate campanile, dates from 1844, and the bridge with three stone arches over the Teviot from 1864. A conservation area, Denholm was the birthplace of the poet and oriental scholar John Leyden (1775–1811), who helped Scott collect material for *The Minstrelsy of the Scottish Border*, became a judge in India and caught a fatal virulent fever while on a visit to Java.

The ruined nearby mansion of Cavers House had its square tower built for Sir Archibald Douglas on the site of an older castle dating from the twelfth century. Far to the south lies the lonely village of Newcastleton, on the banks of Liddel Water. This planned village with a gridiron street pattern was the work of Henry, third Duke of Buccleuch. Its extreme isolation has made it particularly vulnerable to twentieth-century depopulation, but there is a late twentieth-century plan to turn it into a luxurious and well-equipped holiday centre. Its lonely situation in the clean air of the rolling Border hills would certainly seem to make this Liddesdale outpost, in the once much fought-over country of the Armstrongs and the Elliots, ideally suited for such a purpose.

Peeblesshire has the 'feel' of a Border county, although its lands were buffered from the raw disadvantages of life along the English frontier. The village of Carlops, half of which is in Midlothian, stands on the North Esk, and was founded as an eighteenth-century weavers' community. It features in Ramsay's pastoral ballad-opera *The Gentle Shepherd*. Further south, on the Edinburgh to Moffat road, lies West Linton, in the shadow of the Pentland Hills. Its main street follows the curve of the Tyne Water. Its village green forms a centre-piece that, on summer Sundays becomes a sheet of gleaming metal, the control of the parking of Edinburgh's Sabbath-day motorists being a problem the village has not managed to solve. It is a straggle of a place, built to no fixed plan. The statue of a woman on the village pump was carved by James Gifford—'Laird Gifford'—in 1666, and represents his wife.

On the road from Edinburgh to Peebles lies Eddleston, built in 1785 on the left bank of Eddleston Water. It is a conservation area. Of the neighbouring mansions, Patmore is famous—or infamous, if you prefer—as the birthplace of William Forbes Mackenzie, the man who, in 1852, secured an Act of Parliament that

The village of St Abbs,
Berwickshire, sheltered
beneath the rocky
promontory of St Abb's
Head

Lauder, Berwickshire,
looking towards the
Tolbooth

Polwarth Church, built in 1703 by the first Earl of Marchmont, the father of Lady Grizel Baillie

Earlston, Berwickshire, on the Leader Water, traditionally associated with Thomas the Rhymer

Ancrum, Roxburghshire, on the River Ale, once on the path of the northward route into Scotland, and used by the Duke of Hertford in 1545

Denholm, Roxburghshire, birthplace of John Leyden, once had a stocking-weaving industry, and is one of the few Scottish villages with a village green

Newcastleton, Roxburghshire, the principal settlement of Liddesdale, planned as a handloom weaving village in 1793 by the third Duke of Buccleuch

Dirleton, East Lothian, is dominated by the ruins of its twelfth-century stronghold

A picturesque corner of Stenton, East Lothian, with remains of the saddle-backed tower and Norman doorway of the old church

The attractive Preston Mill, near East Linton, on the River Tyne, restored by
The National Trust for Scotland

Athelstaneford, East Lothian, named after the tenth-century Saxon king, Athelstan, and claimed by some to be the birthplace of Sir David Lyndsay. The Reverend John Home once lived in the 1583 manse

Gifford, East Lothian, an eighteenth-century village with fine views south to the Lammermuirs, and once famous for Gifford paper

Inveresk, Midlothian, established on the site of a Roman camp, is now a well preserved seventeenth- to eighteenth-century village

Temple, Midlothian, on the steep banks of the South Esk, has a thirteenth- and fourteenth-century church once a seat of the Knights Templar

shaped the subsequent habits of Scottish drinking. He may have got the solution wrong—the closing of pubs on Sunday was surely an uncivilized gesture, not remedied until 1977—but he was moved to action by a degree of alcoholism in Scotland far worse than anything then to be encountered in England.

Traquair is worthy of mention, even though it is no more than an attendant hamlet upon Traquair House, the oldest continually inhabited dwelling-house in Scotland. The house of Traquair looks rather like an old French château, albeit Scottish in style, with harled walls and corbelled turrets. Once, the Tweed flowed by the walls of an older Traquair; but when James Stuart began building the present house in the seventeenth century, he had the river diverted to a new bed a quarter of a mile away. The first Earl of Traquair supported, after a fashion, Charles I, yet kept his gates shut to Montrose after the disaster of Philiphaugh. Now, the great gates are said to be permanently shut. Two reasons are given. According to the first, following the visit of Prince Charles Edward Stuart in 1745 they are only to be opened again when a Stuart king sits once more upon the throne in London. The second cause of closure is that after they gave passage to the cortège of the Countess of Traquair, the dead wife of Charles, the seventh Earl, he vowed they would stay shut until another countess should enter. The eighth and last Earl died unmarried, leaving the place to his sister, Lady Louisa Stuart, who survived to her hundredth year until 1875, the last of the line. In a room in the peel tower, Queen Mary stayed with Darnley, and a quilt that was embroidered by her 'Four Maries' survives.

Near the house is the "bush aboon Traquair" that inspired a famous nineteenth-century song by J. C. Shairp. The village church has an outside stair leading to the gallery and a vault where traditionally the Stuarts of Traquair are buried. Near to it is the burial place of the Tennants of Glenconner. Further up the burn is their house, The Glen. The Glen was the scene of William Laidlaw's poem "Lucy's Flittin' ", and, of course, the home of a distinguished family at least one of whom was a friend and patron of Burns. Another, rather later, was the witty Margot, who became Countess of Oxford and Asquith.

C

Near the road from Peebles to Biggar lie Skirling and Broughton. The animal painter James Home (1780–1836) was born in
the manse of Skirling. Skirling Church is an old one, restored in
1792 and again in 1893. In the nearby hamlet of Brownsbank, the
poet 'Hugh MacDiarmid' (C. M. Grieve) spent the last years of
his life. On the fringe of Skirling's village green is a wrought-iron
extravaganza of flowers and creatures fashioned by Thomas Hadden for the house of Lord Carmichael, a former colonial administrator, who died in 1926.

Broughton has associations with Lord George Murray, Prince
Charles's Secretary during the 'Forty-five. Lord Murray's home was
burned in 1775, and the estate was bought by the 'hanging' Scots
judge, Robert Macqueen, Lord Braxfield, prototype of Stevenson's
Weir of Hermiston. Broughton Place, which stands on the site of
Murray's house, is the work of the architect Sir Basil Spence. The
pleasant parish church was built in 1804.

3

The Lothians

THE Lothians—East, West and Mid—occupy the south-eastern corner of Scotland. Edinburgh provides their heart, sitting at the foot of the Pentland Hills. Westwards are the mineral workings of West Lothian. To the east lie, in Stevenson's words, the "fat farms" of East Lothian.

East Lothian itself falls readily into occupational divisions. Its coastal belt, studded by fishing villages and small ports that expanded with the development of coal-mining from localized medieval beginnings around Tranent, has become industrialized as it curves round towards Edinburgh, but relaxes eastwards into golfing holiday resorts. The broad howe of its heartland through which the Tyne flows, still carries some of the richest farmland in Scotland. Peaceful villages nestle among the gentle foothills of the Lammermuirs.

Oldhamstocks lies in a dip of a road with a smithy at the foot of it, by-passed by both the A1 route to the north and the Edinburgh–London railway. Oldhamstocks Burn runs across one of its roads. The ford, the village green and the red pantiled cottages that make up the place, seem to reflect the meaning of its ancient name, *Aldhamstoc*, 'old dwelling-place', providing a reminder that this part of Scotland came under Anglo-Saxon domination in medieval times. Once, it was an ancient working village, with its own weavers, blacksmiths, wheelwrights, shoemakers, tailor and saddler. In its present form, it is mainly an eighteenth-century village, a communal pump from this period being one of its features. In the middle of the nineteenth century, its population was just under 800. Now, the figure is down by more than three-quarters. The beautiful old church has a late-Gothic chancel dating probably from the early sixteenth century, the date above the door, 1701, marking a restoration. It shares a minister with Cockburnspath.

Two former incumbents of the parish achieved fame. In 1276 the local minister swore fealty to Edward I in order to get back his rectory. Another minister, Thomas Hepburn—his marriage to a Margaret Sinclair is commemorated by the initials T.H.–M.S. on an armorial stone in the church—distantly related to the Earl of Bothwell, cried the banns in Oldhamstocks for the marriage of Mary, Queen of Scots to Bothwell, and was appointed Master of Requests to Mary, Queen of Scots two days after the ceremony. Later, he assisted her to escape from Loch Leven Castle, for which he was duly tried and convicted. His son, born in 1573, became a traveller and philologist with a European reputation, the author of a Hebrew dictionary and, eventually, Vatican librarian to Pope Paul V. The farmers, weavers, brewers and the others who once worked in Oldhamstocks, are commemorated in the churchyard by carved tombstones showing the tools of their trades. The plain old mercat cross, round which were held fairs under an Act of 1672, has been pieced together again in modern times from the shaft which for long lay in the garden of a house that was formerly the manse. Cromwell slept a night in another house, then the village inn; according to report lying, as he put it, "as sweetly as though I had lain in Abraham's bosom".

In nearby Dunglass, the fifteenth-century church, cruciform in shape with a low tower—originally erected for Masses to be celebrated commemorating the souls of the founder, their ancestors and descendants—came unscathed through both the English raid of 1544 and the upheaval of the Reformation, only to have its west gable torn out in the eighteenth century to make an entrance for carts. It was still thought worthy of detailed description in McGibbon and Ross's classic work *Ecclesiastical Architecture of Scotland* (1896/97, Edinburgh).

Innerwick, said once to have been the scene of a hostile encounter between Wallace and Cospatrick, has a church built in 1784. The main interest of the village today is the prospect of its two ruined castles, standing on either side of a divide half-a-mile away. Innerwick Castle belonged to the Stewarts, then to the Hamiltons, ancestors of the Earls of Haddington. The Master of Hamilton and eight of his friends defended it, unsuccessfully, against Somerset in 1548. Thornton Castle, across the glen, defended on that occasion by Lord Home, met with a similar destructive fate.

Whitekirk's church of St Mary was built near the site of a supposed holy well. It gained its wider reputation in 1274 when Black Agnes, the resolute Countess of Dunbar who defended Dunbar Castle against Edward I until further resistance became pointless, hurt her hand while escaping by boat to Fife. Because of bad weather, she had to put ashore at Fairknowe, as the district was then called. On the advice of a hermit, she drank the water from a certain well, assured by him of a cure if she were sufficiently faithful. The cure effected, she reported the 'miracle' to Andrew de Foreman, Prior of Coldingham, and in the following year built and endowed a chapel on the very spot where the cure had taken place. Miracles then followed thick and fast, particularly successful being the cure for barrenness. A shrine to the Virgin Mary was in due course erected. In 1413, more than fifteen thousand people from many nations came as pilgrims, among the visitors in 1430 being the Italian Aeneas Sylvius Piccolomini, who journeyed to Scotland to visit the court of James I.

Aeneas Sylvius arrived under storm-tossed circumstances. In the midst of a North Sea gale he vowed to walk barefooted to the Virgin Mary's nearest shrine if she would ensue his deliverance from wind and waves. Arriving safely at Dunbar, Aeneas walked the seven snow-covered miles to Whitekirk, an act of piety to which, in later life as Pope Pius II, he attributed his severe rheumatism. Other distinguished pilgrims included James I's widow, Queen Joan, and James IV.

No trace of the miraculous well now remains. Nor is there trace of the interior or roof of the original church, for in 1914 it was set alight by Suffragettes. They left a piece of paper pinned to the chancel timbers, declaring: "By torturing the finest and noblest women in the country you are driving more women into rebellion. . . . Let McKenna, Asquith & Co., beware lest they break that last barrier." Restored by Sir Robert Lorimer, the church was reopened in 1917, and is now the dominating feature of this village of cottages grouped now around the meeting-place of four roads.

On the hill behind the church, the Covenanter Blackadder held his last conventicle. North of the church is a two-storey tithe barn dating in part from the sixteenth century, the only example of its kind left in Scotland.

Tyninghame, 'the hamlet on the Tyne', in no small measure owes its environmental loveliness to the Binning Woods, made up mainly of oaks planted by the sixth Earl of Haddington in 1705 on what had hitherto been moorland. It was visited by Sir Walter Scott. Sadly, the old trees mostly disappeared during the 1939–45 war, although substantial replanting has since taken place. Tyninghame grew up beside Tyninghame House, a seat of the Earls of Haddington refaced with red sandstone in 1829 by the architect William Burn. Although the village is no longer occupied, as it was originally, solely by estate workers, it is essentially an eighteenth-century planned village, its cottages set against ordered squares and lawns. Near the house are the remains of the twelfth-century parish church of St Baldred's. Queen Victoria drove through the grounds of Tyninghame on 26 August 1878, finding them "really beautiful, reminding one of Windsor". Many have opined that the stretch of river from Tyninghame to the coast is one of the finest pastoral scenes in all Scotland.

Travelling north—leaving to the right the breezy double-bayed town of North Berwick, on its promontory, marking the southern limits of the estuary of the Forth—we come to Dirleton, a picturesque village dominated by its Norman castle of the de Vauxs. In 1298 this castle resisted siege by Edward I, although it later fell to the militant Bishop Anthony Bek of Durham. It faced fire again in 1650, when the mosstroopers resisting Cromwell were battered to surrender by Monk's army.

The dominating feature of the castle is the great circular Drum Tower in which may still be seen the original hall, an impressive six-sided room with a vaulted ceiling, a huge fireplace and four large windows. It is probably the oldest of its kind in Scotland. Associated with the castle is a sixteenth-century arch and a bee-hive-type doocot.

The village itself, designated an outstanding conservation area, clusters round two triangular greens. Its Gothic Revival church, retaining the Archerfield Aisle from the earlier church of 1664, stands at the north corner of the smaller green.

In the sixteenth century, when the Ruthvens owned Dirleton, it was offered as a bribe to Logan of Restalrig for his help in the Gowrie Conspiracy. "I care not for all the other land I have in the kingdom if I may grip it," said Logan, "for I esteem it the pleasant-est dwelling in Scotland." But the Gowrie Conspiracy against James VI failed, and another hand did the gripping. Two of the Ruthven sons died in the fracas at Perth. When news of what had happened reached their mother at Dirleton, she, whose husband had been beheaded at Stirling fifteen years before, fled on foot to Berwick with her two remaining sons in an attempt to reach England. But they were rounded up not far from the castle walls, and James VI gave Dirleton to Sir Thomas Erskine, the man who had killed one of the Ruthvens while that assailant was actually struggling with the king. Sir John Nisbet of Dirleton was the author of an import-ant legal work, *Doubts and Questions*, which once led an English Chancellor to observe that Nisbet's doubts were better than most people's certainties.

Aberlady was once a fishing village and, under its old name of Luffness, harbour for the town of Haddington. It lies on sand-fringed Aberlady Bay. The old church near the shore has been re-stored. It has a fifteenth-century tower and contains on its west wall a memorial by Canova to Lady Elibank, who died in 1762, a marble angel holding a torch above an urn. The inscription, written in English by her husband, was reputedly translated into Latin by Dr Johnson, one curiously erroneous and untranslatable phrase be-ing attributed to the mason's difficulties with Johnson's handwrit-ing rather than to any defect in the Doctor's grasp of Latin.

The Elibank seat, Ballencrieff, is now an impressive ruin, as is that of nearby Redhouse. Gosford, the eighteenth-century seat of the Earl of Wemyss in which William Young, the architect of Glasgow's City Chambers, had a hand, survives, as does the Hope family's seat of Luffness.

Port Seton, Prestonpans and Cockenzie, lining the coast, could scarcely any longer be termed villages. The power station of Cockenzie, webbed at the heart of a maze of apparently unsynchronized pylons and transmission lines, dominates everything around it for miles. Prestonpans, like Cockenzie once famous for its salt pans, formerly had two harbours; Acheson's Haven, reputedly built by ancestors of the American politician Dean Acheson in 1526, and Morrisonhaven, used for the export of coal from Tranent. Today, Prestonpans is remembered because of Adam Skirving's song "Hey, Johnnie Cope", celebrating the Battle of Prestonpans, at which Prince Charles Edward Stuart outwitted the unfortunate English commander, Sir John Cope, who thereupon beat an undignified retreat. On the other side of that historic skirmish, Colonel Gardiner of Bankton (now a ruin, destroyed by careless farmworkers in a fire just as it was about to be restored) was shot in the back, then fatally wounded in an assault by a man with a Lochaber axe and carried to the manse of Tranent to die.

From the steeple of the church of Prestonpans, built in the sixteenth century, young Alexander 'Jupiter' Carlyle watched the battle, and vividly recorded his impressions in his *Autobiography*, one of the most forceful pieces of personal diary writing in Scottish literature.

Associated with the village of Preston, which lies adjacent to the former burgh, is the strange story of Lady Grange. Preston House, long since ruined, became the home of Lord Grange, the Honourable James Erskine, fourth Earl of Mar. Grange married a Miss Chiesley, who came of a colourful family, her father having murdered the Lord President in an Edinburgh street. Twenty years after the marriage, Lord and Lady Grange separated, he paying her £100 a year to stay forever apart from him. She, however, apparently returned to Edinburgh to try to persuade him to take her back so that she could see her children.

One day in 1732, a party of Highlanders entered the Edinburgh house where she was staying, seized and gagged her, then moved her north by stealthy stages until she was secretly shipped from

Loch Hourn to St Kilda. On that desolate wind-swept rocky bird-sanctuary she remained virtually imprisoned for six years. Meanwhile, Grange gave out that his wife had died, and celebrated her funeral with pompous rites, himself the chief mourner.

In 1740, however, a letter written two years earlier by Lady Grange reached the hands of the Lord Advocate. Even this revelation of her capture did not bring about her rescue, for those without influence found justice a wanchancy business in the eighteenth century! The unfortunate lady was moved to Skye where she died in 1745, while her dissolute husband, exposed at last, calmly claimed that his action in organizing the kidnapping had been in his wife's best interests. More probably, his shocking act was designed to prevent her knowing and talking too much about the Jacobite intriguing in which increasingly he was becoming involved.

To the south of Preston Church stands Hamilton Dower House, Renaissance in style, dating from 1628 and built for Sir John Hamilton, possibly by the same architect as Heriot's Hospital, Edinburgh. The Dower House has been restored by The National Trust for Scotland. Northfield House, otherwise known as Magdalens or Hamilton's House, built about the same period, also survives. Later developments, however, have made these buildings now of interest individually rather than as part of an integrated village context.

Preston Tower, the fifteenth-century home of the Hamiltons, was burned in 1544 by Hertford and 1650 by Cromwell, and once again, accidentally, in 1633. Not long before its final destruction—it is now a poor ruin—its Hamilton owner added a two-storey house to the top of the tower in order to increase his accommodation.

Preston's seventeenth-century mercat cross—a shaft supporting a unicorn, standing in a drum with steps leading up to a walled platform—is one of the finest to survive in Scotland. Worn and down-at-heel, Preston and its neighbours are examples of villages encrusted by environmentally dilapidating change; villages which only just manage to retain identity by virtue of a few individual buildings and their historic-cum-mythical associations rather than as a result of the widespread conservation of their fabric.

Inland from the coast, the pleasant village of Spott is remembered for a strange case of murder. In 1570, the ambitious incumbent of the parish church, the Reverend John Kell, decided that his wife, Margaret Thomson, was his social inferior and would injure his career. One Sunday morning he strangled her and hung her up on a hook. He then entered his church and preached what seems to have been regarded as the most eloquent sermon he ever delivered. Great was his grief when the supposed suicide was discovered. His tender conscience, however, proved too much for him. Shortly afterwards, he confessed his crime to his incredulous colleague of Dunbar, and was in due course tried and hanged in Edinburgh's Grassmarket, a striking example of those who, as the distinguished twentieth-century forensic expert, John Glaister, once observed, failed to recognize that "there are better ways of getting rid of one's wife than murder".

Stenton, a conservation area village which has managed to retain both its eighteenth- and early nineteenth-century airs, has more to commend it environmentally, grouped around its village green and possessing two smaller subsidiary greens. Near the East Green stands the Tron, once used for the weighing of wool at Stenton Fair. It was restored in 1970. Daw's Well stands at the edge of the West Green. At the north end of Main Street, which is lined with pantiled single- and two-storied cottages, is the Rood Well.

Stenton's original church, only the saddle-backed tower of which remains, was replaced by a Gothic edifice in 1829, again the work of the prolific William Burn. The former manse, built in 1782 and rebuilt in 1820, is still a handsome dwelling. Outside the village—which, like others in the district, has a history of involvement with so-called witchcraft—is a well covered by the replica of a cardinal's hat, and believed to date from the fourteenth century. The nearby house of Biel is said to owe assurance of its continuation to a succession of proprietors remembering to keep this covering in good order. In 1707 Biel belonged to Lord Belhaven, whose great anti-Union speech in the last Scottish Parliament proved of no more avail than the eloquence of his friend Fletcher of Saltoun, incorporating union being a pre-arranged party deal and not subject to reasoned argument, like so many political decisions in our own day. Nearby is the little house of Ruchlaw, bought in 1950 by Dr O. H. Mavor ('James Bridie', the playwright) who died before he was able to move into it.

Up the hill road to the south lies Pressmennan, an artificial stretch of water damned up in 1819. It is sometimes said to share with the Lake of Menteith the distinction of being Scotland's second and only other lake. However, most nineteenth-century writers refer to it as Pressmennan Loch.

Between Stenton and Traprain—the hilly site of a treasure-trove of silver objects dating from about A.D. 500 and uncovered in 1919—lies Whittinghame, the roofed remains of its fifteenth-century tower now a museum. Here, reputedly under the bough of its ancient yew-tree, Bothwell came from Hailes Castle in the company of Maitland on a January day in 1567 to discuss with the Earl of Morton the proposed murder of Queen Mary's husband, Darnley. A. J. Balfour, one-time Prime Minister, had his home in the newer mansion of Whittinghame.

The ruins of Hailes Castle, from which Bothwell rode out to attend his conspiratorial meeting, date back in part to the thirteenth century. Hailes stands on a rocky eminence above the Tyne a mile west of East Linton. The parish church, Prestonkirk, was built in 1770 and added to in 1824. It is said to have been erected on the site of a church at which St Thenew, the mother of Kentigern or Mungo, used to worship. St Mungo supposedly gave the charges of Prestonkirk, Tyninghame and Whitekirk to St Baldred, to whom Prestonkirk was at one time dedicated.

The first, and one of the last, watermills in Scotland, is at East Linton, preserved now by The National Trust for Scotland, its pantiled conical roof a favourite subject for photographers. Nearby, in the house of Phantassie, John Rennie, the builder of canals and bridges, was born in 1761.

By its very name Athelstaneford reminds us of the long Saxon domination of East Linton. The place is said to be called after a Saxon king, Athelstan, killed in battle in the ninth century. It must once have been a singularly pretty village, but although it has been thought worthy of designation as a conservation area, only its older core remains more or less unspoiled.

Two of the incumbents of its church achieved literary fame. The Reverend Robert Blair (1699–1746), author of that lugubrious long poem *The Grave*, became minister here in 1731 and wrote his mournful epic in the manse. William Blake thought sufficiently highly of the words to illustrate it in an edition of 1808. It has been said to have inspired Edward Young's scarcely less uniformly pedestrian *Night Thoughts*.

Blair was succeeded by the Reverend John Home (1722–1808), a man of considerable individuality, as his portrait by Raeburn testifies. After fighting on the Hanoverian side at Falkirk, Home spent eleven years at Athelstaneford, where he wrote his tragedies of *Agis* and *Douglas*. The latter, staged in Edinburgh, led to the enthusiastic cry from the gallery "Whaur's yer Wullie Shakespeare noo?" Though history has shown the Bard of Avon's position to have been largely unaltered by that event, Home's *Douglas* is still occasionally revived. It inspired Burns to pen the astonishing line "Here *Douglas* forms wild Shakespeare into plan" and its first production gave rise to considerable clerical pother. 'Jupiter' Carlyle was hauled before the General Assembly simply for attending one of the performances, though his forceful defence of his action did much to break the grip of the anti-stage clerical party on the theatre. Home, however, decided to resign his charge, becoming private secretary to the Earl of Bute and later tutor to the Prince of Wales.

At the western border of the fertile central district of East Lothian lies Ormiston. From a small hamlet, it was dignified into a planned village by John Cockburn of Ormiston (1685–1758). Cockburn's idea was to encourage tenant farmers to build handsome two-storey houses fronting a broad grass-fringed and tree-lined street, their lands running to the rear of the dwellings. Up from England he brought Lewis Gordon, who not only re-designed the village, using a fifteenth-century cross as the village centre, but gave advice on the enclosure of Cockburn's lands, the original boundaries of which are conserved to this day. Cockburn was a pioneering agriculturalist, introducing the potato to East Lothian as well as the Swedish turnip, the Swedish name, *ruta baga*, giving rise to the Scots word 'baigie', still colloquially used in some parts of Scotland to describe the purple-cheeked variety of turnip. His *Letters to his Gardener*, republished in our own day, make interesting reading.

Cockburn, who founded the Society of Improvers of Knowledge of Agriculture, inherited the old house of Ormiston, whither George Wishart had come on foot in a night of "vehement frost" in December 1545. After family prayers he retired to bed, pronouncing the words "God give quiet rest". But soon the Earl of Bothwell was knocking at the door, demanding that the laird should yield up Wishart. The earl promised Wishart safe conduct before being given custody of the preacher, and then delivered him to Cardinal Beaton who had been waiting meanwhile at nearby Elphinstone Tower. Within a few months Beaton watched Wishart burn in the streets of St Andrews, an event soon avenged when Beaton himself was murdered in his own castle.

Covenanters are said to have held conventicles under the wide spread of the ancient yew-tree, which stands not far from the ruins of the original house. Cockburn, however, built himself a splendid new house, described by one unsympathetic to Georgian architecture, Sir Thomas Dick Lauder, as being in the "tea cannister" style. Unfortunately, this improving laird did not long enjoy his new mansion, having overspent himself in carrying to fulfilment his numerous schemes. He died in London, George, his son, becoming the last of the line. The estate was bought by the Hopetouns. The house fell a prey to dry rot after the 1939–45 war and is now a ruin, though one of its walls is incorporated in an adjacent modern house, built for Mr and Mrs John Busby by Crichton Lang of Ian Lindsay and Partners. In the orchard are the remains of the old church where both Wishart and Knox preached. A brass plaque adorns the wall tomb of Knox's pupil Alexander Cockburn of Ormiston, its Latin inscription allegedly composed by George Buchanan.

Mining had come to rural Ormiston by the end of the eighteenth century. A hundred years later, the place had turned into a mining village, serving five nearby pits. In the 'sixties of the present century, pit closures took away its livelihood, though some miners from the gaunt two-storey miners' rows, built half a century ago at the west end of the village, still travel to nearby pits.

The older part of the village is now a conservation area, the tree-lined streets and the dignified elevations still preserving their aura of order, in spite of gaps and insensitive infilling. A memorial commemorates the birth in the village of Dr James Moffat (1795–1883), the missionary who paved the way for Livingstone in Africa. Off the road that separates village from hall lies the home of the Lauders of Fountainhall. The second Sir John Lauder became a judge with the title of Lord Fountainhall, leaving behind, as well as legal writings, his chatty *Journals and Observations in Public Affairs from 1665–1676*.

Neighbouring Pencaitland has also managed to preserve its rural aspect, principally because the older part of the village lies along the wooded banks of the Tyne. By the edge of the water is a fine church with an octagonal spire and a slated cap crowning its tower. Outside there is an interesting stair, and inside a thirteenth-century choir aisle.

The magnificently Renaissance Winton Castle, built in 1620 for the third Earl of Winton, has Tudor chimney-stacks. New Winton is a planned cottage hamlet that later development has left more or less to its own charms. East Salton, situated on a steep slope, once had as its parish minister Gilbert Burnet (1643–1715), who eventually became Bishop of Salisbury. To his old parish Burnet bequeathed 20,000 Scots merks, to posterity his highly readable *History of the Reformation*.

The boy Andrew Fletcher, who hailed from Saltoun Hall which stands below the village, was influenced by Burnet. Fletcher became a member of the Scots Parliament and the leader of those who saw the long-term threat to Scotland's traditions and prosperity of the fully incorporating Union that befell her, in spite of the eloquence of Fletcher, Belhaven and their friends. He is now most generally remembered by a usually erroneously-quoted remark, that, in fact, goes: "I knew a very wise man, so much of Sir Christopher's sentiments that he believed if a man were permitted to make all the ballads, he need not care who should make the laws of a nation."

The village of Bolton might perhaps not of itself be particularly worthy of mention were it not that in the centre of the church-yard Burns's mother, Agnes Broun, lies buried, along with poet's brother Gilbert, who had been farm manager to Mrs Dunlop at the farm of West Mains. After it was sold in 1804, he became factor to Lord Blantyre. Gilbert brought his mother to live in the house of Grant's Braes, now no longer standing.

Garvald as it is today dates mostly from the 1780s, its houses using locally-quarried red sandstone topped with an assortment of slated and pantiled roofs. The red pantiles, so typical of East Coast villages, were originally imported from the Low Countries although later they were manufactured in Scotland. Garvald village lies hidden in a narrow valley of the Lammermuirs, beside the curiously named Papana Water. Its original church belonged to the Cistercian priory of Haddington until the Reformation, but was replaced by the present T-shaped building in 1829, using the main ground-plan of the older building. By the entrance is a stone sun-dial of 1633.

Near Garvald is Nunraw (Nun's Row). The original castle was built on land granted to the Cistercian nuns when they settled there in the reign of Malcolm IV. In James II's time they were granted a royal charter to "fortifie the nunnery", being allowed to have "guns aye loaded to shoot at our aulden enemies of England". In 1563 the last prioress, herself a Hepburn, gave Nunraw to Sir Patrick Hepburn. The Hepburns then built themselves a Z-plan castle, capable of defending itself but relaxed enough to allow such luxuries as painted ceilings. Restored in 1863 and added to in the 1880s Nunraw became a Cistercian monastery in 1945, the first to be re-established in Scotland since the Reformation.

On Easter Monday seven years later, the Order cut the first sod in the building of their new abbey of Sancta Maria, a task origin-ally not due to be completed until 1987. The BBC despatched me to Nunraw to record an interview with the abbot. Being a fine day, I drove down with my wife, only to discover that the monks be-longed to a silent order and that women were not permitted beyond the outer guest-room. In these circumstances the best that could be done was what in pre-television days used to be called a 'colour piece'; not really a difficult word-task, in view of the pastoral beauty of the setting.

Further along the Lammermuir foothills, a once equally peaceful village tucks itself away. This is Gifford, which claims to be the birthplace of John Knox, never having entirely resigned its claim in favour of Haddington. Gifford, however, was indubitably the native village of Dr John Witherspoon, first President of America's Princeton University and the only clergyman to sign the Declaration of Independence.

Gifford is a planned village that replaced Bathans when, in the seventeenth century, it was cleared from the grounds of Yester House. The twelfth-century Yester Castle has long since vanished, except for the arch-roofed underground chamber known as Goblin Ha', where Scott's Marmion came to meet the fairy warrior who, long before, had battled with Alexander III. The Ha' is supposed to have been built by people not of this earth, to the orders of Sir Hugo de Gifford, the Wizard of Yester.

We are on surer architectural ground with Yester House, begun in 1699 by James Smith and Alexander McGill, but completed more than a century later to plans by William and Robert Adam and Robert Brown. The Gifford lands passed by marriage to the Hays, later the Marquesses of Tweeddale. At the moment of writing, Yester is the Scottish home of the composer Gian Carlo Menotti.

The orderly main street of the village runs from the market cross right to the gates of Yester. The church, built in 1700, shows Dutch influence. It has its Tweeddale gallery and anteroom opposite the seventeenth-century pulpit taken from St Bathans when the fifteenth-century former parish church became the Tweeddale burial-vault. The appearance of the village, with its vernacular houses mostly of two storeys, cannot have altered much since the early nineteenth century. Well laid-out with trees—Beechback Wood, indeed, is said to contain the tallest beech in these islands —Gifford retains a closeness with its peaceful origins and natural surroundings few other villages can claim.

The villages of West Lothian and Midlothian are more difficult to categorize. Almost the whole of the Forth estuarial coastline has developed in such a way as to turn one-time royal burghs like Musselburgh, as well as planned residential outposts of Edinburgh like Portobello, into suburbs of the capital. Granton has certainly long since outgrown village status. So, too, has Cramond, although it still preserves its village heart.

While the identity which Musselburgh seeks staunchly to preserve is that of a burgh rather than a village, half-a-mile up-hill from its main street lies the village of Inveresk. In the 1890s it was dubbed 'the Montpelier of Scotland', and is, indeed, still a fairly superior village, its Georgian houses preserving a well-cared for elegance. On the west side of the street, the high walls of the Manor House and of Halkerston assert their continuing privacy.

Halkerston must be one of the oldest houses in the village, standing near the site of a former church dedicated to St Michael and credited by legend with having been built from the ruins of a Roman station. George Wishart preached to its congregation in 1545 two months before his martyrdom. With its four aisles it must once have been a magnificent building. Ironically, the most distinguished minister of the parish, Alexander 'Jupiter' Carlyle (1722–1805), described by Scott as "the grandest demi-god I ever saw", spent much of his long ministry striving to secure the building of the present, rather uninteresting four-square church.

In the churchyard, which must be one of the most beautiful in Scotland, there is a mound reputed to have been the site of a Roman temple. Here, Cromwell is said to have sited a battery, as earlier, Somerset had called a conference around it before the Battle of Pinkie. Roman remains have been discovered here, some as long ago as 1565, when an altar came to light. Urns, bricks, medals and coins have since been found. In 1783, the remains of a hypocaust were uncovered in the grounds of Inveresk House.

Similar in character, though now indubitably a village within the city of Edinburgh, Duddingston stands on a hill at the south-east of the Queen's Park, near Duddingston Loch. The loch, a bird sanctuary, has been many times painted, nowhere more vividly than in Raeburn's portrait of the Reverend John Thomson skating. Thomson (1778–1840), a native of Dailly, in Ayrshire, spent most of his ministerial life at Duddingston. A strong if eccentric character, he was loved both for himself and because of the admiration his landscape paintings inspired among people far beyond the bounds of his parish. His paintings have continued to excite the admiration of lovers of Scottish art, although unfortunately the quality of his pigment has caused many of his pictures to darken, raising doubts about their prospects of long-term survival. Nevertheless, there is a spontaneous vigour and directness about Thomson's Scottish landscapes which few other contemporary artists captured, and is certainly not to be found in the stylized romantic landscapes of the nineteenth century.

He features in a dialogue between 'Christopher North' (John Wilson) and James Hogg, the 'Ettrick shepherd', in North's *Noctes Ambrosianæ*:

> North   Mr Thomson of Duddingston is now our greatest landscape painter. In what sullen skies he sometimes shrouds the solitary moors!
>
> Shepherd   An wi' what blinks o' beauty he aften brings out frae beneath the clouds the spine o' some pastoral parish kirk, till you feel it is the Sabbath.
>
> North   Time and decay crumbling his earth seems to be coming again the very living rock—and we feel their endurance in their desolation.
>
> Shepherd   I never look at his roarin' rivers, wi' a' their precipices, without thinkin' somehoo or ither, o' Sir William Wallace. They seem to belang to an unconquerable country.

Thomson's painting of Fast Castle has a special interest, in that it is associated with Scott's novel *The Bride of Lammermoor*.

Duddingston's Sheep's Heid Inn is said to date from the fourteenth century. One of the oldest inns in Scotland, it has enjoyed among its patrons Mary, Queen of Scots, James VI and Bonnie Prince Charlie. To the east of the village, Duddingston House was built in 1768 by Sir William Chambers for the eighth Earl of Abercorn. Also just outside the village is Nairne Lodge, to which Caroline, Lady Nairne came in 1806 as a bride. With, among others, "The Laird o' Cockpen", "The Land o' the Leal", "Will ye no' come back again?" and "Charlie is my darling" to her popular credit, more of her songs are still sung in Scotland than those of any writer other than Burns. Although she was living at Nairne

Lodge when Scott came to visit Thomson, she herself never actually met the author of *Waverley*, preferring to preserve her anonymity, after the fashion of women writers of the times.

Lasswade, on the banks of the North Esk, has outgrown the village status it enjoyed when Thomas de Quincey came to live in a cottage a mile away, near Polton Station. Here he made his home from 1840 until his death in 1859. The cottage opposite Dunesk House, to which Walter Scott brought Charlotte Carpenter as his bride in 1798, has been much enlarged. During the six years the couple stayed here, Scott began to establish his reputation as a poet, and was visited by a still greater poet, William Wordsworth, along with his sister Dorothy. Lasswade is said to be the prototype of Gandercleugh in Scott's *Tales of my Landlord*, in which Jedediah Cleishbotham, schoolmaster and parish clerk of Gandercleugh, and Peter Pattieson, the supposed recipient of the tales, are made frequenters of the Wallace Inn. The church, built in 1793 but much reconstructed in 1886, contains in one of its aisles the burying-place of the Melville family. The body of Henry Dundas, first Viscount Melville, the colleague and friend of Pitt and from 1775 to 1805 "the uncrowned King of Scotland", lies here. In a smaller arched aisle lie the earthly remains of the poet William Drummond of Hawthornden, whose beautiful house, still containing the little room which was once his study, overlooks the Esk from a rocky cliff. William Tennant, whose *Anster Fair* may have provided Lord Byron with a model for the stanza so brilliantly used in *Don Juan*, was schoolmaster at Lasswade from 1816 to 1819.

Just outside Lasswade, Melville Castle was built in 1786 to designs of John Playfair. By his marriage to the daughter of the laird of Melville, the estate came into the possession of Henry Dundas, first Viscount Melville (1742–1811) one of the most powerful ministers in the Government of the younger Pitt. Scott, then still living in Lasswade, wrote in "The Grey Brother" of Melville Castle's "beechy grove". "Willie", the wooer celebrated in song, had some difficulty in deciding which of the lovely ladies of Melville he wished to wed, so departed uncommitted, "boots an' spurs an' a' ", amidst maidenly tears with the promise to come back and wed them all. The castle is now an hotel.

The village of Newbattle, which lies in a valley of the South Esk, exists because of its abbey, once a powerful monastery founded by David I's Cistercian monks in 1146 but latterly a seat of the Marquises of Lothian. In 1937 the eleventh Marquis of Lothian presented it to the nation to become a college for adult education.

The abbey was burned by Richard II in 1385, restored to its former beauty, then burned again in 1544. The last Abbot of Newbattle, Mark Kerr, became a Protestant at the Reformation, and as was common with such converts of convenience, was created Commendator of Newbattle. His son became Lord Newbattle, later Earl of Lothian; thus a Cistercian monastery was turned into an aristocratic seat. Until 1952, when it was blown down in a gale, the largest beech tree in Britain grew in these grounds. Queen Victoria inspected the tree in 1842, as doubtless did George IV during his visit twenty years earlier.

The centre of the village is now a conservation area. The hotel opposite the entrance to the abbey was once the first halt for Edinburgh–London coaches. The church was put up in 1726. Its predecessor had as an incumbent from 1641 to 1653 Dr Robert Leighton, later Archbishop of Glasgow. The manse is an older building, dating from 1625.

A little to the south of Newbattle, where the Dalhousie Burn joins the South Esk, stand Cockpen Church and Dalhousie Castle, the latter the ancient seat of the Ramsays. The old House of Cockpen, once occupied by the famous laird whose self-satisfaction is celebrated in comic verse, stood near the Esk, to the east of the castle.

The conservation area of Carrington begins at the junction of the Cockpen to Carrington Road and the track leading to Whitehill Aisle. The village of Carrington is situated about a mile and a half from Gorebridge. A hamlet rather than a village, its houses are vernacular in style, its church, dated 1710, having pointed latticed windows. It is unfortunately redundant, its future at the moment of writing uncertain. Four roads meet in Carrington, and the village has developed in a linear form to accommodate them, the slight curve of Main Street providing that sense of enclosure so pleasant in a village. Trees at either end help to strengthen this sense of entity. The local authority does not intend to allow any alterations to the frontages of Carrington's cottages and houses.

The little village of Borthwick has a nearby Romanesque church, almost destroyed by fire in 1775. Fortunately the fifteenth-century barrel-vaulted aisle survived. It includes a painted effigy of a Lord Borthwick in full knightly accoutrements. The aisle and portrait are now in the modern church. The most important feature of Borthwick, however, is Borthwick Castle, dated 1430. Mary, Queen of Scots and Bothwell were blockaded there in 1567, after their marriage, by Morton and the rebel lords. They escaped separately, Mary disguised as a page-boy. The castle was besieged by Cromwell in 1650, and damaged a little by one of his cannon. During the Second World War the public records of Scotland were deposited in the castle. It has now been restored as a modern management training and conference centre.

Crichton, still further east, is another hamlet that is also a conservation area. It lies two miles east of Gorebridge and was originally built as a 'ferm toun' to house workers for Crichton Mains Farm. There must once have been a link between Crichton Church and the castle. The church is one of the few remaining pre-Reformation churches in the Lowlands. It was built in 1499 by Sir William Crichton, Chancellor of Scotland under James I and James II, in thankfulness for all the manifest deliverances vouchsafed to him, and dedicated to Glasgow's patron saint, Mungo. It was restored in 1899.

The castle, on the other hand, is a ruin, below which the Tyne flows distantly through the trees. What is left of the building dates mostly from the fifteenth century. The oldest part contains a dungeon, the only entrance to which is through the roof. Named Massie More, it echoes colloquially the ancient name for Saracen castles in Spain. Scott's *Marmion* contains a picturesque description of the castle:

> Crichton! though now thy miry court
> But pens the lazy steer and sheep;
> Thy turrets rude and totter'd keep

Have been the minstrel's loved resort.
Oft have I traced within thy fort,
Of mouldering shields the mystic sense,
Scutcheons of honour or pretence,
Quarter'd in old armorial sort,
Remains of rude magnificence. . . .

Within these walls the plan was discussed for curbing the power
of the Douglases, an exchange of resentments and suspicions that
led to the Black Dinner in Edinburgh Castle, when the sixth Earl
of Douglas and his brother, Fleming of Cumbernauld, were dragged
from the monarch's presence and summarily beheaded. From Crichton, the second Earl of Bothwell marched with his men to Flodden
and death on the field of battle. To Crichton in 1562 came Mary,
Queen of Scots, for the wedding of her bastard brother, Jamie
Stuart. It is said, too, by what W. Gordon Smith calls "bydand
myth", that part of her honeymoon with Darnley was spent within its walls.

Another picturesque hamlet, Fala Dam, three-quarters of a mile
from the A68, is grouped around a narrow bridge of sturdy distinction. The dwellings, of which Falaburn House is the largest,
range in date from the middle of the eighteenth century to the
middle of the nineteenth, and also enjoy the protection of being
a conservation area.

On the A68 lies the old linear village of Pathhead. Its main street
has several houses of distinction, and a particularly good example
of sensitive infilling. Yet like so many of these small villages, it is
its group value which has won it conservation area status. This is
also true of nearby Ford, which has grown up around Ford House,
a typical seventeenth-century laird's dwelling, L-shaped in pattern,
vernacular in style, with crow-stepped gables and an octagonal
turnpike stair tower. Its neighbour, Mill House, is a dignified three-
storey eighteenth-century dwelling. Visually linking Ford and Pathhead is the pastoral view across the meadow of Telford's fine
Lothian Bridge.

Down the A7 is the road which leads through Middleton and
Heriot to Stow, on the banks of Gala Water. This little place, the
Townfoot area of which is really a Victorian linear village, possesses

a Gothic Revival style church, St Mary of Wedale, with an impressive spire, put up in 1876. The memory of the ruined older church survives only through a built-up window dated 1660. Stow also has an arched pack-horse bridge, one of only three survivors of its kind in Scotland.

Nearer to Edinburgh lie three villages, all conservation areas and all worth a visit. The village of Temple has become famous because it was the home during his last years of the painter Sir William Gillies (1898–1973). The village fabric was one of his favourite subjects, the gentle slope of the village street familiar now in many varied lights and conditions of weather to people who have never actually been there. At the foot of the village, a group of red-roofed cottages cluster a grassy bank, and below, in the glen through which the South Esk flows, is the church. This has been adapted to become the home of the glass-engraver Alison Kinnaird and her husband, Robin Morton. Here, too, stands the roofless frame of its fourteenth-century predecessor. Originally called Balantradoch, the Knights Templar built a chapel here, thus giving the village its present name. The surviving ruin, however, was probably built for the successors to the Knights Templar, the Knights of St John. Rosebery, from which the Earl of Rosebery takes his title, and Arniston, seat of another branch of the Dundas family, are both nearby.

Nearer the Pentlands lies Howgate, two miles south-east of Penicuik, a little village with the curiously-named eighteenth-century Howgate Mouth as its most important building, and the old Howgate Inn, formerly a coaching stop on the route between Edinburgh and Peebles, its most popular howf. The linear slope of the village relates to the former turnpike road. It is now a conservation area.

Further west lie two villages celebrated in Allan Ramsay's ballad-opera *The Gentle Shepherd*. The tiny village of Ninemileburn lies next to Habbie's Howe.

> Between twa birks, out o'er a little linn,
> The water fa's, and makes a singan din;
> A pool breast-deep, beneath as clear as glass,
> Kisses, with easy whirls, the bord'ring grass.

This little hamlet, on the Logan and Glencorse Burn, may indeed be the source of the poet's inspiration and certainly a place:

Where a' the sweets o' spring and summer grow.

Carlops stakes its claim by naming its hotel after the poet. Newhall, on the North Esk, also claims the honour, and is supported by the testimony of Tytler of Woodhouselee, who claimed to have heard Ramsay recite his poem before it was printed. But Habbie's Howe is the more picturesque of the two, lying beneath its grey crags and the tree-lined Howe Burn. Newhall, in Peebleshire, claims the poem's:

... blasted tree,
With faulded arms and half-raised hook ...

though the ash tree was associated in Ramsay's day with Carlops House rather than the village, which was not founded until rather later.

The Pentland Hills form a divide down Midlothian, the villages to the west having for the most part felt the influence of the industrial developments of West Lothian. But Ratho, an L-shaped village and a conservation area, has an original core, a timber-ceilinged kirk which in part dates from the thirteenth century, and a Georgian laird's house built in 1803. Ratho Hall, a little off the road, dates from the late eighteenth century, and possesses some fine ceilings. The cottages of Main Street have a satisfying group entity, and a Georgian bridge crosses the Union Canal, giving fine views to either side.

Kirknewton has swollen in recent years from being a linear village to quite a sizeable place, with the acquisition of local authority housing and accommodation for members of the armed forces. At the time of writing, its main street, with its rows of eighteenth- and nineteenth-century cottages, is badly in need of restoration, the residential life of the place having been drained from the old heart to the new areas. For group value it has been made a conservation area so that its future preservation may be assured.

Kirknewton lies three miles east of Mid Calder. There are, in fact, three Calders in the valley of the River Almond. Collectively they once used to be known as 'the country of the Red Mountains'

since at West Calder, Dr James 'Paraffin' Young (1811–83) set up
the first shale mine in the 1850s, establishing a market for shale oil
only curtailed by the eventually cheaper extraction possibilities of
petroleum. The red bings are now being grassed over, but the processes of industry still dominate the countryside. The once-rural
village of Livingston has been transformed into one of Scotland's
New Towns. In the midst of all this, only an ancient home or two
remains; most notably, Calder House, seat of the Torphichen family,
whose great hall is said to have echoed to the verbal thunder of
Knox when he took his first communion there in 1556 (an event
celebrated by Sir David Wilkie's picture in the Scottish National
Gallery); Houston House, near Broxburn, built by Sir John Shairp
in 1601; and Kirkhill, now a farm, but once a mansion and the
home of the eccentric eleventh Earl of Buchan, who regarded himself as a patron of Burns and built in his grounds a curious solar
system, only a solitary stone of which still remains.

The heart of Mid Calder is a conservation area, the east side of
Market Street and the north side of Bank Street marking the
original village. Across the former county border lie Torphichen
and Uphall, both conservation areas. Torphichen (after the Gaelic
Torr-fithicheann, 'the hill of the raven') lies just west of the hill
of Cairnpapple, where excavations, begun in 1947, revealed a
burial place in use from about 2000 B.C. until the Bronze Age,
more than a thousand years later.

The village of Torphichen has as its centre-piece the Preceptory
of the Knights of St John, who made it their headquarters in Scotland from 1153. Chancel and nave are gone, but the vaulted transept survives, with traceried windows and a graceful surmount-
ing central tower still retaining its spiral staircase. There is a
monument to the penultimate preceptor, Sir Walter Lindsay, who
died in 1586, "a valiant capitane by sea and land". The last preceptor, Sir James Sandilands, did the prudent thing, turned Re-
former, and received what was left of the estates as a temporal
barony, together with the title of Lord Torphichen.

Much of the interesting character of the village has been eroded
by the building of council houses, or by the creation of gap-sites
which sooner or later will need careful infilling. Still, the approaches

are pleasant, and enough remains to justify its designation as a conservation area. Henry Bell (1767–1830), who pioneered steam navigation in Europe, was a native of the parish.

Uphall, once also involved in the paraffin industry, has lost much more of its character, but the old village centre, focusing on Oatridge Hotel, deserves, and is getting, conservation protection. The policies of Houston House provide a pastoral approach to the place, which also borrows visual strength from the proximity of the Brox (Badger's) Burn to the main street.

Kirkliston retains its square. Its outstanding buildings are its thirteenth-century parish church and Castle House. Blackness, on the estuary of the Forth, has its ship-like castle, but has suffered from unsuitable housing development near the area of its ancient harbour.

On Lanarkshire's border with Peeblesshire there is an interesting group of villages. 'The hill of the seer' may provide the titular origin of the high village of Dunsyre, in the valley between Dunsyre Hill and the Black Mount, near the banks of the South Medwin Water, which forms the south-western extremity of the Pentlands. Agricola's army is said to have passed through the place *en route* from Tweeddale to the Roman camp of Cleghorn. Dunsyre was much involved as a place of safe retreat for the Covenanters. Among them was William Veitch, tenant-farmer at Westhills, who was caught after Rullion Green. At his trial he was successfully defended by the advocate who later rose to the bench as Lord Minto. In later years Veitch joked to Minto: "Had it no been for me, my Lord, ye'd still be writing papers at a plack a page." Minto is said to have retorted: "Had it no been for me, the pyets wed hae pyked your pow on the Netherbow Port." The equally famous Covenanter Donald Cargill preached on Dunsyre Common in 1669.

A hill path leads from Dunsyre to Dolphinton. In the churchyard—the church itself is old, dating probably from the early seventeenth century in its present form—lies Major Learmont of Newholm, commander of the Covenanting horse at the skirmish of Rullion Green in 1666.

Newbigging would scarcely be worth the mention did it not possess an ancient market cross, thought to date from the thirteenth century. Dunsyre, Dolphinton and Skirling all allege that, rightfully, the cross belongs to them.

Carnwath House, where Prince Charlie supposedly slept, is now a golf club-house. Cowthally Castle, a Somerville seat, provided James V with a mistress, Katherine Carmichael, on whom he first set eyes at a wedding party there. Carnwath Church, dating from 1867, incorporates the beautiful north transept of the collegiate church built by Lord Somerville in 1424. Many of the Somervilles, as well as the Lockharts of Lee, are buried here.

4

West and South-West

ALTHOUGH Lanarkshire's eastern border fringes the hilly country of western Peeblesshire, and has the Lowther Hills as part of its boundary with Dumfriesshire, Lanarkshire's long eastern frontier, from the Nith valley northwards, leads almost to the boundaries of Glasgow (which it once encompassed, until the major cities achieved independent administrative status). Lanarkshire's traditions, for the most part, have looked west rather than east.

There are, first, the villages of the high lands; Leadhills, the second highest village in the Lowlands, built on a windy ridge of the Lowther foothills above the Glenconner Water, was the birthplace of Allan Ramsay (1686–1758), the first important poet and editor in that phase of Scottish literary history known as the Eighteenth Century Revival. William Symington (1764–1831), whose experimental steamboat once carried Burns as a passenger on Dalswinton Loch, was also a native, his connection celebrated by an obelisk. Lead may have been worked here by the Romans. Lead and gold were certainly mined in Stuart days, the crowns of James V and his queen being made with gold from this hilly place. The village, as it now stands, consists of one long sloping street with a church at the summit.

Just over the border with Dumfriesshire, Wanlockhead, thirty feet nearer to Presbyterian heaven, is related to Leadhills by a comity of interest in mining. The Wanlockhead gold mines were worked as early as 1572, though by about the middle of the eighteenth century lead was usually the mineral being brought up.

The mines closed in 1914. In 1732, the miners formed a society "for the purpose of purchasing a collection of books for our mutual improvement"—Burns was connected with two similar village societies—and by 1853 the collection was housed in its own building. The village has mostly been converted to holiday homes, or to provide student accommodation for the Field Study Centre in the old library. The church, built in 1848, replaced an eighteenth-century one.

Elvanfoot, near the junction of Elvan Water and the Clyde, stands on the edge of some of the wildest Lowland country in Scotland. Its red sandstone church, dating from Edwardian times, has a stained-glass window commemorating the actor-manager Wilson Barrett, whose company, like that of his son after him, provided a middle-class drama need nowadays satisfied by television. Westwards through the 'Lang Glen'—a road often traversed by Burns, who is said to have frequently stopped off at the little white tollhouse of Glen Eith—is the Daer Valley water scheme, which helps to quench the thirst of Glaswegians. The Daer Water is, in fact, the principal contributory head water to the River Clyde, although the river takes its name from the smaller Clydes-burn, which flows to the east above Elvanfoot. In this particular hilly stretch, three rivers have their source, and are commemorated in an old rhyme:

> Annan, Tweed and Clyde
> Sprang from ae hillside;
> Tweed ran, Annan wan,
> Clyde fell and brak its neck owre Corra Lynn.

North towards Tinto lie Crawford and Abington, both now by-passed by the beautifully contoured though notoriously mis-driven A74 north–south road. Crawford suffered in the days when the main road ran so near to the village that its peace was disturbed by having continuously to cater for large numbers of travellers. A Lindsay should have a special interest in Crawford. On the opposite bank of the Clyde stand the ruined walls of Tower Lindsay. Crawford Castle, to give it its more usual name, was the seat of the Lindsays from the twelfth century until 1488. In 1397, Sir David Lindsay of Glenesk became an earl and chose the name of

Crawford for his title. Adherence to Catholicism during the reigns
of Mary and James VI resulted in the title going to a younger
branch of the family, the Lindsays of the Byres. (The sixth Lord
Lindsay of the Byres helped pressurize Mary, Queen of Scots into
resigning her crown.) It was not until 1848 that James, the
seventh Earl of Balcarres, successfully established his claim to the
earldom of Crawford.

Nearby Crawfordjohn is memorable because its lonely position,
surrounded by hills from which flow Duneaton Water and Snar
Water, led Dorothy Wordsworth, passing through the place in
1803 in company with brother, William, and Coleridge to comment: "Scotland is the country above all others that I have seen
in which a man of imagination may carve out his own pleasures.
There are so many inhabited solitudes." The dour vernacular
seventeenth-century house of Gilkerscleugh, like too much that
was savable in parts of our heritage, has been allowed to fall into
decay in recent times.

I once found myself by accident, having lost my way, in the
village of Roberton, a casual little sprawl on a beautiful hillside.
It has neither important buildings nor historic significance, so I
simply record the delight it gave me. Further down the valley, the
road from Lamington to Biggar traverses some of the loveliest hill
country in upper Lanarkshire.

The old part of Lamington is a conservation area. It contains
the parish church of St Ninian, rebuilt in 1828 but retaining a
bell dated 1647 and a fine Norman arch. Curiously enough, Burns
disliked the church, or was perhaps just travel-weary on an exposed
day, when he wrote:

> As cauld a wind as ever blew,
> As cauld a kirk, but in't but few,
> As cauld a minister's ever spak,
> Ye'ee a' be het or I come back.

At Lamington, the Clyde begins to settle into its valley. Woods
and hills—notably, Tinto—provide a back-drop to the village.
North of the village is the ruined tower of Lamington. Surrounded
on three sides by the Clyde it is all that is left of the once strong
fortress known as the 'Bower of Wandell'.

Cutler is one of the most attractive villages in Lanarkshire. The parish church was founded in 1170 by the monks of Kelso, and the shape of this building is marked by a walled enclosure east of the present nineteenth-century church. The village lies along Culter Water and has a nominal relationship with the highest of Lanarkshire's hills, Culter Fell, almost 2,500 feet high, from the summit of which Clydesdale, Tweeddale and Peeblesshire can be seen magnificently to sprawl away.

Well-conserved Biggar, though it looks like a town and probably now is, preserves the 'feel' of a large village. With its wide tree-lined main street and its freshly-painted shops and hotels, it wears an air of county prosperity. It has one fine building, the well-restored sixteenth-century parish church of St Mary, which contains within its walls parts of the twelfth-century church of St Nicholas. It also possesses a splendid museum of Biggar bygones. Biggar Water, when in flood, is said to achieve the feat of flowing both ways, distributing its superfluous waters to the Clyde in the west and the Tweed in the east. Dr John Brown (1810–82), the essayist author of *Rab and his Friends*, was a native of the place.

Carstairs village—not to be confused with the railway junction a mile away, now the point where the Edinburgh train to London and the South is joined to (or detached from) the main Glasgow train—has had much of its character eroded. Covington, a hamlet rather than a village, has a beautifully isolated setting, with its ruined castle, church and working farmhouse grouped closely together.

At the foot of the brae that slopes from the plateau on which Lanark stands down to the banks of the Clyde, lies the 'model' village of New Lanark, founded in 1783 by one of Glasgow's most famous and industrious citizens, David Dale, in partnership with Richard Arkwright. The object of this development was to establish a cotton-spinning community on socialist lines, to be, it was hoped, the admiration of the world. Arkwright and Dale soon parted company—allegedly over the siting of the bell which was to summon the villagers to work and play! So in 1799 Dale was joined by Robert Owen, who married Dale's daughter, making his home at nearby Braxfield House, now fallen into decay but once the home of Scotland's hanging judge, Lord Braxfield.

To cotton-spinning was added net-making and sail manufacture after 1881, when the Gourock Ropeworks Company took over the village. But the mills finally closed in 1968, leaving this village of red sandstone houses and mill-buildings, some of them seven storeys high, with its chapel, schoolhouse and centre for character improvement to moulder, like the discarded machinery now rotting within sight and sound of the Clyde. A housing association was set up. It achieved some impressive restoration, but ran into financial trouble. The Scottish Civic Trust, in company with government and the post-reorganization local authorities (taking over the good work from their predecessors) has helped establish a local administration under a full-time director. Slowly, the task of restoration and of attracting suitable craft industries is gathering momentum, the ultimate aim being to make the village of New Lanark as commanding a tourist attraction as New Harmony, in America, which Owen set up after he left Scotland in 1827.

Not all of Lanarkshire's industrial villages either enjoyed such idealistic motivation behind their construction or have such a beautiful and fundamentally unspoilable natural setting. Heavy industry is still a dirty business, and was much more so in the days of reeking coal-fired factory chimneys. The scarring of industrial Lanarkshire through rapidly expanding unplanned industrial development in the latter half of the nineteenth century has left Central Scotland a scarred legacy of dereliction that has proved one of its most severe economic handicaps in the twentieth. Mining settlements like Wilsontown and Coalburn, through no fault whatever of those who have lived, or still live in them, must surely vie with each other for the dubious honour of being Scotland's least attractive village!

Further down the Clyde, the fruit-growing villages blossom the valley in early summer. Crossford was visited by Scott on his way to see ruined Craignethan, the Tulliebardine of *Old Mortality*. It was rebuilt by James Hamilton of Finnart, known as 'the Bastard of Arran' and the only Scottish architect to have been beheaded, though for political treachery rather than for professional short-

Torphichen, West Lothian, much mutilated in recent years, still has parts of the fifteenth-century preceptory of the Knights Hospitallers of the Order of St John of Jerusalem

Leadhills, Lanarkshire, one of the highest villages in Scotland, surrounded by hills yielding lead and gold from Roman times and the birthplace of the poet Allan Ramsay

Wanlockhead, Dumfriesshire, a former gold- and lead-mining village set bleakly in the southern uplands

New Lanark, Lanarkshire, the former
cotton-milling village founded in 1783
by David Dale. It is now being
restored by New Lanark
Conservation and Civic Trust
and the local authority

Kilbarchan, Renfrewshire, a former weaving village with a weaver's cottage
museum and a Steeple of 1755, housing a statue of the piper, Habbie Simson

Kilmaurs, Ayrshire, built round the fifteenth-century collegiate church and once famous for horn spoons, cutlery and bonnets

A quiet corner of Symington, Ayrshire, now spoiled by modern fringe building

The mining village of Tarbolton, Ayrshire, at the Water of Fail. Burns was once an enthusiastic member of The Bachelors' Club (*left*)

Straiton, Ayrshire, on the Girvan Water, is a charming eighteenth-century agricultural village with a pre-Reformation church

Dunure Castle, a Kennedy stronghold, stands above a shore of particular interest to the geologist and lapidary

Dunure Village, Ayrshire, still has its little fishing fleet based on its attractive harbour

Portpatrick, on the west coast of the Rinns of Galloway, once the port for
Northern Ireland until replaced by the more sheltered Stranraer in 1849

Isle of Whithorn, Wigtownshire, once an island community, now a coastal
village with a twelfth-century chapel and a harbour

Carsethorn, Kirkcudbrightshire, on the Lower Nith estuary enjoyed a brisk schooner trade until the 1920s. Many emigrants in the 1850s left its ruined jetty for Canada, Australia and New Zealand

New Abbey, Kirkcudbrightshire, a village of great beauty by the foot of Criffel, is dominated by the warm red stone of Sweetheart Abbey which rises above the whitewashed cottages

comings. Craignethan was eventually restored to his son; here, legend insists, Queen Mary spent part of the week before the disastrous Battle of Langside.

If, indeed, she did, then she must have looked out on a green and fertile strath, though doubtless there would be other things on her mind. Twenty-five years ago, a journalist, Theo Lang, was able to write: "Here is the fabulously rich fruit-garden of Scotland. . . . The market gardeners of Lanarkshire have carpeted the valley floor with their neat plots, continuing, it is said, a tradition of the Romans . . . and between the orchards are the glasshouses, such glasshouses as one will see nowhere else in Britain."

So it was then. But today, the glint of the sun on vast expanses of sloping glass no longer sends blinding semaphores across the valley. Changed economic circumstances and altered growing methods have reduced this picturesque sight, though the orchards themselves still flourish.

Just under three miles down the valley is Rosebank, whose Popinjay Hotel—'popinjay' is the Middle Scots word for 'parrot'—is a reminder that here archery once flourished, the wooden popinjay being the customary target. Nearby Dalserf has a kirk with an unusual ogee-capped belfry.

Douglas, which in past times gave its name to one of the most powerful houses in Scotland, still has some late eighteenth-century houses in its high street. Passing across the border of Renfrewshire, there is Carmunnock, a once-charming but now much altered village on the periphery of Glasgow.

It once served Castlemilk House, where Mary, Queen of Scots is said to have arrived from Craignethan on the night before the Battle of Langside, fought on 13 May 1568. "Washing and dressing white goods for the hotels and warehouses of the city" was given as "the principal occupation of the place" at the end of the nineteenth century. Its hilly, rural charm survived into the 'fifties of the present century, when neglect, the destruction of its manse and other savaging developments, took their toll. What is left has been designated a conservation area. If a sensitive policy of infilling is enforced, something of its older charm might yet be consolidated.

E

By far the finest of Scotland's planned villages is Eaglesham. It was founded by the twelfth Earl of Eglinton in 1796. To achieve his dream, he demolished the old village, of sufficient importance to have acquired by Act of Parliament a weekly market during the reign of Charles II. The earl intended not the charming village we have today, with its long sloping green flanked by two rows of neat houses, but a small cotton-spinning and weaving town. Indeed, a cotton factory was built near the top end of the meadow, but was burnt and never replaced.

Eaglesham Parish Church, part of the original building, has an eagle on its spire, although the probable definition of the name is from the Gaelic *eaglais*, a church, rather than from the bird. The church has the coolly elegant yet simple interior that builders of eighteenth-century places of worship in Scotland could so often achieve.

The other public building of importance is Polnoon Lodge built in 1732 by the ninth Earl of Eglinton as a hunting lodge, but sharing its name with the Montgomerie's ruined castle of Polnoon, or Poinon, said to derive from the ransom or poind money Sir John Montgomerie got for capturing Hotspur at the Battle of Otterburn. While the old castle is a dilapidated ruin by the banks of the White Cart, the lodge has been carefully restored by the former Renfrew County Council, and is now in use as housing for old people.

The Eaglesham houses on either side of 'The Orry', as the meadow is called—simple terraces of traditional Scottish domestic architecture, for the most part—directly front the street, their gardens, originally *lang riggs*, running to the back. They are protected by outstanding conservation area status. Long before the concept of the conservation area was formulated, special measures had been taken to protect the unique character of a village now much sought after as a healthily airy dormitory suburb of Glasgow. It achieved prominence of another sort in 1941, when our fortunes in the Nazi war were at their lowest ebb. A fighter plane crashed in a nearby field, and an astonished Scottish farmer found himself receiving into captivity the sadly deluded Rudolf Hess, who had baled out, believing that by having a conversation with the then Duke of Hamilton the war could be brought to a speedy end.

Another Renfrewshire village with qualities quite its own is Kilbarchan. Like every Scottish place-name with a *Kil* prefix, here there must once have been the cell of a holy man, in this case St Barchan. But it was for weaving, piping and poetry rather than piety that the place was to become known, even though it was from the Knoxes of nearby Ranfurly Castle that the family of John Knox is supposed to have been descended.

The streets of the village, High and Low Barholm, Shuttle Street, Steep Street, are, so to say, gathered together by the focal point of The Steeple, built in 1755 by the then laird, one Major Milliken, who made his fortune trading to the West Indies. It was intended to be a schoolhouse and meal market. The Steeple and adjoining village hall of 1782 have now been well restored. There is a bell in the tower.

Other public buildings include the much altered former United Presbyterian Church, now Kilbarchan East Church, and the old parish church, now the church hall, though it is a much better building than its more elevated newer neighbour.

The little cottages mostly date from the eighteenth century, although the houses belong to the early decades of the nineteenth. At the height of the prosperity of the cottage-weaving industry, as many as a thousand looms could be heard clacking busily in Kilbarchan. Something of this former way of life is preserved by The National Trust for Scotland in their fascinating Weaver's Cottage Museum in the village. Residential pressures and local authority policies should lead to the restoration of the cottages still in bad repair, and to suitable gap-site replacements.

In the graveyard of the old parish church Habbie Simson, the sixteenth-century Piper of Kilbarchan, is buried. His statue, a bronze copy of the wooden model of 1822 by Archibald Robertson, is in a niche of The Steeple not far from the ground where St Barchan's Fair was held annually, and at which Habbie's playing was much admired.

His continuing importance, however, arises not so much from his musical ability as from the fact that a local poet, Robert Sempill of Beltrees, in 1640 lamented Habbie in a mock-elegy, "The Life and Death of Habbie Simson, the Piper of Kilbarchan", reviving an old stanza-form stemming from troubadours but later to be developed by the writers of the Eighteenth Century Revival—notably Ramsay, Fergusson and Burns—to such an extent that it was dubbed 'Standard Habbie':

> At fares he play'd before the spear-men,
> All gaily graithéd in their gear, man;   (*dressed*)
> Steel bonnets, jacks and swords so dear then
>   Like ony bead:
> Now wha will play before such weir-men
>   Sin' Habbie's deid? . . .

> And at horse races many a day,
> Before the black, the brown, the grey,
> He gart his pipe, when he did play,   (*caused*)
>   Baith skirl and skreed:
> Now all such pastime's quite away
>   Sin' Habbie's deid.

Another planned weaving village, Houston, dating from 1771, replaces an older estate settlement lower down the Houston Burn. Originally, the new village had two streets—Miliken Street, now South Street, and North Street—on either side of the burn, the latter an early nineteenth-century development. The consequences of the collapse of cottage weaving, some nineteenth-century extensions and several contemporary residential 'estates', have altered its original character, though enough of the old village survives to justify its status as a conservation area. The mercat cross, with a headpiece dated 1713, has a fourteenth-century plinth. Cochrane's Place and Kerr's Lane have good examples of eighteenth-century domestic building.

Houston and Killellan Parish Church, containing monuments to John of Houston and his wife, who died in 1456, was built in 1874, St Fillan's Roman Catholic Church in 1841. Of its Victorian mansions, Woodend in Houston Road, a Tudor Revival house from about 1850, has an eighteenth-century stable block and a pair of overwindows from the Old Glasgow College, Houston House replaced the former Houston Palace. Part late seventeenth century—

the doorpiece is dated 1625—it was altered in 1872. A family of MacGuires befriended the mother of the laird of Houston, General Macrae, while that worthy was pursuing a profitable Indian career. Having no son of his own, the general persuaded a MacGuire to change his name of Macrae, so that he could inherit. This Mac-Guire/Macrae pulled down most of the palace in 1780, and two years later thrashed the footman of Ramsay of Banff outside an Edinburgh theatre. Ramsay not unnaturally, objected. He was challenged to a duel by Macrae, who killed his opponent on Musselburgh Links, and had to flee the country. Macrae died twenty years later, still an outlaw.

Near Houston, set on a small hill, is Barochan Cross, a Celtic monument now so weathered that it should be re-located under protective cover.

Weaving was also the staple trade of Lochwinnoch, along with tanning, thread- and candle-making. It has many gap-sites. A few have been skilfully infilled, but more require sympathetic treatment.

As its name suggests, Lochwinnoch looks out on its own stretch of water, Castle Semple Loch. Noteworthy is its main street, composed mostly of early nineteenth-century buildings in the local vernacular, some with characteristic gable chimneys at the front, an unusual octagonal parish church, dating from 1806 and the ruined collegiate church, founded by the first Lord Sempill, who fell at Flodden. The second Lord Sempill, an early supporter of Mary, Queen of Scots until the death of Darnley, bought the nearby lands of Beltrees and gave them to his son John, who married one of the queen's 'Four Maries', Mary Livingston. Of their union John Knox wrote, with characteristic charity: "It was weill knawin, that schame haistit marriage betwix Johne Sempill, calit the Danser, and Marie Levinstoune, surnameit the Lustie."

Their son, Sir James, wrote a series of political pasquils in verse. His son was poet Robert, already referred to as the author of "Habbie Simson". Francis, Robert's son, wrote, among other things, another enduringly popular Scots song, "Maggie Lauder". But with him, husbandry fared less well than poetry. The Macdonalds took over the estate, and built an elegant mansion in 1735 unfortunately burned down in the 'thirties of the present century. Castle Semple is also a ruin, though a consolidated one. The Muirshiel Country Park can be approached from Lochwinnoch.

In Strathgryfe—formerly the name for the whole of Renfrewshire—there are two villages that have somewhat outgrown their status, Bridge of Weir and Kilmacolm. Bridge of Weir straddles the Gryfe Water. High quality tanning has provided its livelihood for centuries, although since the middle of the nineteenth century its residential suburb of Ranfurly has outgrown the old village.

Kilmacolm, on the other hand, leans upon a hillside in moorland country once a haunt of Covenanters. The place itself derives from the Gaelic *Cille ma Coluim*, the cell of Columba, though more probably it was a cell or church set up by one of his followers rather than a place he himself founded. The parish church, built in Gothic Revival style in 1833, incorporates a thirteenth-century chancel in the vestry.

There are two other interesting points about this church. It was the last Church of Scotland kirk to have its incumbency filled under the old patronage system: and it is the burial place of the Cunninghams, Earls of Glencairn. The ninth Earl, whom Burns saved from the oblivion that has overtaken the others, died at Falmouth. Burns wrote of his patron's demise:

> The mother may forget the child
> That smiles sae sweetly on her knee;
> But I'll remember thee, Glencairn,
> And a' that thou hast done for me!

It was an author, R. B. Cunninghame Graham, a descendant of this last Earl, who unveiled the commemorative brass tablet in the church.

Kilmacolm became a dormitory village for Glasgow towards the end of the ninteenth century. Great houses were built on the hillside—a hillside swept by air so healthy that it once had a hydro where the wealthy came to cure their ills, real or imaginary—many of them by famous architects.

The most famous of all these villas is Charles Rennie Mackintosh's Windyhill, put up between 1899 and 1901. Although it has suffered more severely from internal alteration than Hill House, Helensburgh, its exterior is virtually unaltered, and it finds its way into Mackintosh articles in many languages and histories of architecture. Also in Houston Street is Rowantreehill, the work of Mackintosh's disciple, James Salmon. Salmon was fairly active in Kilmacolm, his other houses including Miyanoshta, now the Roman Catholic Bishop's house, in Porterfield Street; Hazelhope in Gryffe Road; Den o' Gryffe, in Knockbuckle Road; and Nether Knockbuckle nearby. Mackintosh himself had a hand in the lodge of Auchenbothie House, on the Port Glasgow Road, and also built Cloak, formerly Mosside, on Cloak Road. Auchenbothie House itself is the work of William Leiper, now an old folks' home. Leiper was also the architect for the flamboyant Gothic Revival Church of St Columba's, put up as St James's in 1902.

The best of several houses by another architect active locally, J. Austen Laird, is perhaps Greystones, in Houston Road.

Between the junction of the Green Water and Blackett Water humped walls raise up the grass, all that survives of the old castle of Duchal. Here, Marion Boyd bore a son to James IV. The boy grew up a favourite pupil of Erasmus, and with that rapid elevation which was often the lot of royal bastards, became Archbishop of St Andrews at the age of eighteen. There, he founded St Leonard's College, which he left to go to Flodden Field, where he died alongside his father. Duchal House in its present form dates from about 1768, although part of an earlier house of 1710 was incorporated in the south-west wing.

The old Duchal Castle had a family ghost. According to the medieval *Chronicle of Lanercost*, this ghost differed from many in that it made itself readily available during daylight, when it would jeer from the castle outbuildings at those going about their daily business. If it was shot at and hit, the arrow turned molten. One night, legend relates, the Knight of Duchal's eldest son took on the demon in personal combat. Next morning his dead body was found amid the wreckage of the hall. The ghost was never seen again.

Two of Renfrewshire's villages look out upon the Clyde. Langbank, in its present form a mid-Victorian village, is largely a dormitory for Glasgow and Greenock. It carried the coastal traffic through its centre until the construction of the present M8 motor-way, which lies between the village and the River Clyde. It looks across to Dumbarton Rock, standing sentinel in front of the town of Dumbarton, at the mouth of the Leven. Finlaystone House, above Langbank on the Port Glasgow Road, is a Baronial Revival building with slated corner towers. Probably the main part of it went up about 1760, but it was extensively remodelled and added to by Sir J. J. Burnet in 1893.

Further down the coast, Inverkip looks over the Firth of Clyde towards the Cowal Hills. It, too, suffered environmental damage, and the abandonment of some of its properties, as holiday traffic pushed through it. That traffic now passes along a broad new road between the village and the water; but this relief has been bought at a severe price. Inverkip has become the site of a large power station, completed by the South of Scotland Electricity Board in 1976. The chimney rises above the skyline of the hills, and domin-ates what was formerly an estuary of such scenic beauty as to in-vite comparison with the Italian Lakes.

The marring for ever of this lovely scene provides a monument to the inadequacy of our first quarter-century of mandatory plan-ning. The electricity authorities were presumably well aware of their own growth plan to meet increasing consumption, and the planning authorities no doubt had similar foreknowledge at their disposal. Yet at the outcome of a public inquiry, the then Secretary of State, William Ross, felt obliged to grant permission for this generating station and chimney to be erected at Inverkip rather than at Dundonald—an environmentally preferable site further down the estuary—only because there was no longer time to wait for the radar station at Dundonald to be phased out of use, or to investigate other sites.

Inverkip Castle, a late fifteenth-century tower, stands in the grounds of Ardgowan estate. The mansion house was built in 1798. Dr James Young, the discoverer of paraffin, is buried in the churchyard. The nearby pre-Reformation kirk was once the con-cern of the monks of Paisley. Beyond the seventeenth-century bridge in Shieldhill Glen, nothing remains of the castle of the once powerful Lindsays of Dunrod. The last laird's method of dealing

with inflation was perhaps not such as would make him popular
in the locality:

> Auld Dunrod was a goustie carle
>   As ever ye micht see;
> An gin he wasna a warlock wicht,
>   There was nane in the hale countrie.

> Auld Dunrod stuck in a pin,
>   A bourtrie pin, in the wa;
> An when he wanted his neighbours' milk,
>   He just gied the pin a thraw.

Driving along the coastal road towards Ayrshire, our principal
pleasure is likely to be the view across the estuary to the Cowal
Hills, Bute and Arran, rather than in buildings by the wayside.
The two counties are linked in an odd way, Wemyss Bay being in
Renfrewshire whilst its other half across the Kelly Burn, hillier
Skelmorlie, leads one almost imperceptibly over the old county
boundary. When the development of the steamboat had opened up
the possibilities of the Clyde to tourism one owner of the Kellie
estate had the idea in 1834 of making the place "a Brighton on
the Clyde". He went so far as to re-christen the place 'New Glasgow'. That done, little else happened, and his optimism was not
rewarded.

A later owner of the estates was Dr 'Paraffin' Young, already
referred to. Young was a great admirer of David Livingstone, and
invited the bearers who had brought Livingstone's body to the
African coast to come over to Britain. They then built for Young
a facsimile of the hut in which Livingstone had died. House and
hut were eventually destroyed by fire, allegedly put to the flames
by Suffragettes.

Castle Wemyss was the nineteenth-century red sandstone home
of Lord Inverclyde, whose ancestors were involved in the founding
of the Cunard Line. Anthony Trollope, while a guest of the first
Baron Inverclyde, is said to have written part of his Barchester
saga in the place.

Higher up the hill, at the entrance to Skelmorlie Glen, Skelmorlie Castle looks across the Firth. It is basically a keep of 1502

with a seventeenth-century addition and Victorian alterations, all recently well-restored. The pier at Wemyss Bay, once (but no longer) a graceful edifice leading out into the water beneath an ornamental glass canopy, played an important part in the victory of the railway steamers over the 'doon the watter' boats from Glasgow's Broomielaw, which had originally developed the Clyde trade in pre-railroad days. With the disintegration of the Clyde cruising fleet and changed holiday habits, much of the pier fell into serious neglect, and part of it has suffered fire damage.

Since there are no villages of distinction down the Ayrshire coast, except perhaps West Kilbride with its nineteenth-century high street—though much magnificent scenery and several pleasant little towns—until one moves south of the Heads of Ayr, let us now turn inland.

Dunlop, which stands on the right bank of the Glazert Burn, is famous for two reasons. In the days when Scottish cheeses were still made locally with highly distinctive flavours, one of the most flavoursome was that which bore the name of Dunlop. It is said that Barbara Gilmour, a young woman exiled in Ireland between the Restoration and the Revolution of 1688, which drove out the Stuarts, settled in Dunlop as a farmer's wife. She began to make cheese from unskimmed milk, a process not then known in Scotland. It soon found a wider market. William Cobbett, of *Rural Rides* fame, thought it "equal in quality to any cheese from Cheshire, Gloucestershire or Wiltshire". Now that the majority of Scottish cheeses, like most others manufactured in Britain, appear to be made of a tasteless edible plastic, the strong fame of the true Dunlop is a thing of the past. Not so, however, Burns's connection with the Dunlop family. Mrs Dunlop of Dunlop, his "mother-confidante", to whom he wrote many of his most interesting letters, belonged to a family that owned the lands of Dunlop from 1260 until the middle of the nineteenth century.

What is mainly worth looking at in Dunlop today is the conservation area. It includes Dunlop Kirk, known as the Laigh Kirk, situated in Townfoot, the older part of the village, and in its present form dating from 1835. But it incorporates parts of two earlier churches, the northern aisle dating from 1641. Here are buried many members of the Dunlop family. Nearby, there is a picturesque irregular row of one-storey cottages, fronted by a narrow pavement-lined main street. The two rows on the opposite side considerably add to the pleasing character of the village.

Moving along the road to Kilmarnock and passing through the town of Stewarton, one reaches Kilmaurs, originally Cunninghame, but renamed after St Maure in the thirteenth century. It was created a burgh of barony by the third Earl of Glencairn in 1527, and in addition to its continuing agricultural interests, has been known for its cutlery, once so sharp as to give rise to the saying "As gleg as a Kilmaurs whittle". Incredible as it now seems, in the bad old days of the 'fifties and 'sixties, when local authorities were hell-bent on destroying any part of the heritage that appeared to get in the way of faster progress for motor vehicles, there was actually a proposal to isolate the seventeenth-century Council House and steeple. On the outside of the wall of the Council House hang the ancient jougs, dating, doubtless, from the same period as the mercat cross, though used as late as 1812.

The parish church, originally collegiate, was built in 1404, but rebuilt completely in 1888. The Glencairn burial aisle nearby was put up by the seventh Earl in 1600, restored in 1844, and houses a memorial to the ninth Earl, William, Lord High Chancellor of Scotland, who was buried in St Giles, Edinburgh, on his death in 1664.

Half-way across the moors between Kilmaurs and Fenwick stands Rowallan Castle, the traditional home of the Mures of Rowallan, a Covenanting family one of whose members was the poet and historian William Mure, described by an anonymous contemporary as a man "pious and learned, had an excellent vein of poesie, and much delyted in building and planting". Rowallan provided a 'pulpit' for one of the best known of the local Covenanters, William Guthrie, after he had been ejected in 1664. It was built in the fourteenth century, although there is a twelfth-century date above the doorway, and the ruins of a still older castle survive nearby.

Fenwick—strictly speaking, the combined villages of High and Laigh Fenwick—stands 500 feet above sea level, eleven miles inland from the Clyde. Although it is at the centre of a rich dairy farming area, the once all encompassing moorland is never very far away. Fenwick claims to hold within its parish the graves of more Covenanters than anywhere else in Scotland. A Fenwick man, John Howie of Lochgoin (1735–91) chronicled their actions in his *Scots Worthies*. The church, which stands in the High Town or upper part of the village, was built in 1643, but restored in 1929 after a fire. Affixed to the pulpit is an hour-glass, the replica of a three-hundred-year-old one destroyed in the fire, though contained in the original iron bracket, and housing, it seems, the original sand. Seventeenth-century jougs have survived here too, attached to the church. While their main use was to silence brawling women, it appears that they were also sometimes applied to discourage sabbath-breakers from whatever simple pleasure they might sinfully have indulged in. At Kirton Brae, the cottages of a community of shoemakers have now vanished. John Fulton (1800–53), designer of the Orrery in the People's Palace on Glasgow Green, was a cobbler who taught himself mathematics. In one of these vanished cottages the psalm tune "Martyrdom" was composed by Hugh Wilson.

The Laigh Town was given over to weaving, a cottage industry which here survived into the twentieth century. Fenwick is also credited with establishing the first co-operative society in the world, in 1769. Rightly, Fenwick enjoys the protection of being a conservation area. Though the original rather plain linear village has no listed buildings, it is of typical Scottish construction. Similar protection is afforded to Laigh Fenwick, whose groupings of vernacular and picturesque small houses have been restored with sympathy and charm.

On the other side of Kilmarnock, between the town and the Clyde coast lie three villages of some charm; Dreghorn, Dundonald and Symington. The little cottages that form the old part of Dreghorn look down upon the Firth of Clyde. It is a peaceful bywater, as is the original village of Dundonald. In the distant view stand the ruins of the fourteenth-century castle of Dundonald, allegedly built mysteriously by one Donald Din, but certainly used by the early Stuart kings. Like the former neighbouring house of Auchans, allegedly built with stones from the top storey of Dundonald, it was owned by the Cochrane family. Both buildings are twentieth-century losses.

Robert II died at Dundonald in 1390. Boswell and Johnson visited Auchans in 1773, the Countess of Eglinton, then in her eighty-fifth year, so falling for the Doctor that she called him her "dear son". Boswell said of this former beauty, to whom Allan Ramsay dedicated *The Gentle Shepherd*: "Her figure was magestick, her manners high bred, her reading extensive and her conversation elegant". However, she did have her difficulties. Though she was the earl's third wife, when she produced five daughters one after the other, she found herself faced with the threat of divorce. Her husband having made his dissatisfaction over her failure to produce an heir plain to her, she replied: "Give me back the youth, beauty and virginity with which I came to you, and you may do as you please." But what the earl did resulted in another child, the longed-for son and heir, and marital harmony prevailed.

The classical church in Dundonald village, is the predecessor of which the first Earl of Dundonald was buried, at his own request without monument, in 1686, dates from 1803.

The church at the end of the twisting road to Symington dates basically from the Norman period, although it was substantially remodelled in 1880. In 1919, it was restored as a war memorial. Its black open-beam ceiling is similar to that of the church of the Holy Rood in Stirling.

The old part of Symington has suffered some damage by demolition and unsympathetic intrusion, but now enjoys the advantages of being a conservation area, the windings of the main street and the variation in levels providing distinctive features of interest.

Two villages in Central Ayrshire attract visitors because of their association with Burns. Mauchline has grown into a town, but the old part of it retains the character of a small closed community it must have possessed in Burns's day.

The fifteenth-century tower, built by the monks of Melrose Abbey and known as Mauchline Castle, has a residence attached to it. This was once the home of Gavin Hamilton, Burns's friend and the landlord of Mossgiel. In one of its rooms Burns is said to have written his parody of an "Auld Licht" sermon, "The Calf", and later, to have married Jean Armour. Burns's first home after the marriage in Causeway, now Castle Street, was restored and given in trust to the Glasgow and District Burns Society. It is furnished as it might have been in Burns's day. Also restored is the house next door, once occupied by Dr John Mackenzie, Burns's doctor, and opposite it Nanse Tinnock's, which features in "The Holy Fair". Poosie Nancie's, where the Jolly Beggars forgathered, is still a pub, although the Whitefoord Arms (which Burns preferred, and which stood at the opposite corner) has unfortunately given place to an incongruous shop.

A memorial obelisk by the entrance to the school, celebrating the execution of five Covenanters in 1685, reminds us that the further we travel south-west, the deeper we move into Covenanting country. A still earlier preacher whose word was not to the official satisfaction of his time was George Wishart, who in 1544 found the church door at Mauchline shut in his face and led his congregation out to a nearby moor.

Just as Mauchline was the place of convivial gathering for Burns when farming Mossgiel, Tarbolton had provided a similar service when the Burns family farmed the then sour lands of Lochlea, where William Burnes, the poet's father, died. Tarbolton, which stands near the Water of Fail, though spoiled at the edges with miners' houses, has a plain parish church of 1821, and the long low range of its Black Bull Inn. The fiery prophet-preacher of the Covenant, Alexander Peden (1626–86), was for a time school-master at Tarbolton. Earlier still, Esmé Stuart, Lord d'Aubigny, a nobleman celebrated in verse by William Dunbar, in addition to his title of Duke of Lennox also carried that of Lord Tarbolton.

On 11 November 1780, Burns and his brother Gilbert, with the aid of a few friends, founded 'The Bachelors' Club', a debating society in which issues of the day were earnestly discussed. The thatched two-storey Bachelors' Club is now looked after by The National Trust for Scotland. It was at Tarbolton, too, that Burns became a Freemason, although the actual St James's Lodge, of which he became Deputy Master, has given place to a later building. In it one may see Burns's insignia of office and several documents bearing his signature. John Wilson, a schoolteacher who dabbled in drugs, also lived in Tarbolton, and provided Burns with the subject for his satirical poem "Death and Dr Hornbook".

On the Mauchline road to the east, beside the River Fail, Willie's Mill was the home of William Muir, who took in Jean Armour when she had become pregnant to Burns for the second time prior to her marriage. To the south-east, Montgomerie—formerly the mansion of Coilsfield—employed 'Montgomerie's Peggy', who enjoyed the songs Burns made for her, but not his advances. There, too, he met Mary Campbell, the dairymaid from Dunoon immortalized as 'Highland Mary' and who, if later conjecture be correct, probably enjoyed both. In any case, her death in Greenock, possibly bearing his child, left him free legally to marry Jean Armour. 'Highland Mary' is commemorated by a monument at Failford, where the Fail joins the River Ayr. Although drab, unimaginative council housing—the curse of so many Scottish villages—together with nineteenth-century associations with mining, has deprived Tarbolton of much of what must have been its unified attractiveness in Burns's day, it is still worth a visit.

Sorn has its attractive eighteenth-century bridge and an eighteenth-century church, one of the few in Scotland open generally to the public. Sorn Castle, still lived in, is a Victorian enlargement of a medieval structure. Catrine, built as a small village at the time of the industrial revolution, was the handiwork of Sir Claud Alexander of Ballochmyle. It was begun in 1787. Sir Claud's sister, Wilhelmina, was the haughty subject of Burns's song "The Lass of Ballochmyle". At Catrine, Sir Claud set up a cotton mill with David Dale, the Glasgow industrialist. The grim mill which once dominated the square has gone and given place to trees, flowerbeds and seats. The Alexander home, Ballochmyle House, is now part of Ballochmyle General Hospital.

The most attractive of Ayrshire's villages, however, lie to the south. Three miles east by south of Maybole, on the Dyrock Burn, stands the little agricultural village of Kirkmichael. It has a church built in 1787 dedicated to St Michael. The churchyard gateway, a delightful 'stop' for the eye looking down the village street, has a plain arch curved in the line of a Dutch gable. It is one of the few roofed lych-gates to survive in Scotland. The Dyrock Burn

makes its gentle way towards the Girvan Water, passing under two
pleasing bridges that contribute much to the ambience of this little
village.

In the same parish, the long linear village of Crosshill stands
on the left bank of Girvan Water. Its main street is now a conservation area. Further up the river, in the Carrick Hills, the eighteenth-century village of Straiton climbs up its brae. It can scarcely
have changed over many years, and to me it seems one of the most
attractive villages in Scotland. The Black Bull Hotel carries the
date 1766 on the lintel. St Cuthbert's Church, dating from 1758,
contains a pre-Reformation chantry chapel, believed to have been
founded about 1350 but enlarged during the fifteenth century.
Alterations and additions were made twice in the eighteenth century, in 1813 and in 1901, when the tower was added and a pulpit,
made in Amsterdam of light oak, was installed. There is a wooden
ceiling and a carved frieze, as well as a stained-glass window depicting the four evangelists. The window was installed in 1900 to
commemorate a member of the family of the Hunter Blairs of
Blairquhan, one of whose antecedents was a friend of Burns. The
little cottages, with their colourful gardens to the front, are well
looked after; a conservation area in fact about which the local
authority need do very little, except, of course, deter those who
might in future years seek to spoil its sense of fitness with itself.

In the same parish, though on the other side of the River Doon,
the mining village of Patna has fine hilly prospects. Dailly still
preserves some of its character, with a quirky-looking eighteenth-
century church, in spite of some ugly mining housing. Nearby is
one of the saddest ruins in all Scotland, that of Robert Adam's
great house of Dalquharran, dismantled after the Second World
War; a fate which surely it would not have been allowed to suffer
had its moment of decision come a quarter of a century later.

Hilly prospects are also a feature of two other Ayrshire villages.
Between the coast and the Carrick Hills, in the upper valley of the
River Stinchar, lies Barr, an agricultural settlement seven miles
inland from Girvan. Its original cottages and inns are set pleasantly along the banks of the Gregg Water in magnificent wooded
hill country. The Water of Gregg joins the Stinchar just south of

the Stinchar Bridge, a hump-backed structure dated 1787. Barr-hill, on the road from Girvan to Newton Stewart, is also a hilly village, on the River Dusk. Though it is a mid-nineteenth-century place, its situation and its sense of integrity justify its designation as a conservation area.

Along the Ayrshire coast lies Dunure, one of the last fishing villages of its kind. Its fishermen's cottages, grouped at the foot of a headland, complete with wooden net-drying racks turned towards the harbour, were constructed in 1811. Dunure House, an early nineteenth-century building, stands in landscaped grounds north of the harbour.

Dunure, however, is dominated by the ruins of its fourteenth-century castle, a home of the Kennedys. When the share-out of church lands following the Reformation was in progress, Gilbert Kennedy, the fourth Earl of Cassilis, objected to the grant of the lands of Crossraguel to Allan Stewart, its Commendator. The earl thereupon seized Stewart and carried him to Dunure, where the unfortunate man was roasted on a spit and basted with oil until he surrendered the lands. For this outrage the Privy Council fined the earl two thousand pounds. Stewart, who said that he would "never be able nor weill in my lifetime again", was given a pension by the earl; but the earl kept the lands.

Maidens Harbour, further down the coast, and its row of Scottish fishers' cottages, is also a conservation area, although the surroundings have been spoiled by hutted holiday developments.

The village of Kirkoswald lies on the road from Maybole to Girvan, not far south of the ruins of Crossraguel. Kirkoswald typifies an eighteenth- and early nineteenth-century Lowland Scottish village, with the building line of its whitewashed houses set hard against the pavement, its gardens to the rear. Burns underwent part of his schooling there in 1775, at the house of Hugh Roper, which stands opposite the old kirkyard and has a bronze tablet on the wall. The church in which Burns worshipped was replaced in 1777 by the present building, paid for by the Earl of Cassilis and designed by Robert Adam. The old bell, transferred to the new church, is thought to have been cast in Holland and bears the date 1677. There is a belief that the ancient font, discovered

F

at Chapel Donan near Girvan and now in the kirkyard at Kirkoswald, may have been used for the baptism of Robert, the Bruce.

On surer ground is the association of Kirkoswald with Burns's great narrative poem "Tam O'Shanter". Founded on a Kirkoswald tale, the prototype of Tam was possibly Douglas Graham, who lived in the now demolished farm of Shanter, to the west of the village. James Thom, a friend of Graham's, who occupied the little cottage that is now a museum in the care of The National Trust for Scotland, was a self-taught sculptor from Tarbolton. He carved the figures depicting the famous characters in the poem, which are to be seen today in the back garden of the cottage.

Before we leave Ayrshire for Galloway, two other villages deserve our attention. Colmonell, on the River Stinchar, though not much more than a single curve of cottages, is a conservation area. The predominant physical feature of the place is the conical hill called Knockdolian, probably deriving from the Gaelic *cnoc* 'hill' and *dall* 'to mislead' the feature, it seems, being in former times under bad weather conditions mistaken by mariners for Ailsa Craig, which lies off the coast. Colmonell is also of interest in that it has a rich collection of ruined castles. Kirkhill stands next to the house that supplanted it. Seventeenth-century Knockdolian is also an adjunct to a nineteenth-century mansion. A one-time hiding-place of Bruce, Craigneil, which stands on the hillside across the river from Colmonell, partially collapsed early in the century as a result of quarrying operations. It is the oldest of the three, dating back to the thirteenth century, and was once a prison.

The church at Colmonell, built in 1772, has a kirkyard housing three martyred Covenanters. One of them, Matthew M'Ilwraith, was slain, according to his epitaph, by order of 'Bloody Claverhouse'. He is said to have been shot after a chase from Barrhill, and buried in a shallow grave by his fiancée and another woman, who wrapped him in their plaids. He is supposed to have provided Scott with the prototype of Mucklewrath in *Old Mortality*. Also buried here are the parents of John Snell, who, in 1664, raised a stone over their grave. He himself became the founder of the Snell exhibition from Glasgow to Balliol College, Oxford.

At the mouth of the Stinchar lies Ballantrae. The valley behind is a beautiful one, inspiring Burns to write the song beginning "Behind yon hill where Stinchar flows", the hill being Knockdolian. However, the poetic properties of the word *Stinchar* did not please the poet, so he substituted the name *Lugar* instead, thus transporting the song further north. Literary transposition in reverse was carried out by Stevenson, who used the name of the village for his second greatest novel, *The Master of Ballantrae*. In this case, the vivid action of the story is staged near Borgue, in the Stewartry of Kirkcudbright. While Burns is not known ever to have visited Ballantrae, Stevenson arrived in the village during January 1876. His wife recorded that "the flowing, mellifluous sound of the Master of Ballantrae" seemed to give him "an impression of elegance and smooth simplicity that should suggest the character he meant to depict".

Only a fragment remains of the castle of Ardstinchar, once the home of the Bargany branch of the Kennedy family. It was a family torn by vicious conflict for over forty years, the feud beginning with the roasting of the Commendator of Crossraguel at Dunure and ending in the High Court of Edinburgh in 1611. At one point, to rid himself of his hated rival, the Earl of Cassilis planned to blow up Ardstinchar, but was persuaded from this act of violence by his uncle, who counselled that it would displease the king and involve the deaths of innocent people. In spite of his villainy, whether merely planned or actually executed, the eventual ousting of the Bargany branch left the earl the supreme ruler in Carrick. From this feud Scott took the plot of "Auchindrane", and Crockett used it for his story *The Grey Man*, in which the cannibal Sawny Bean features. Ballantrae, with its breezy views of Ailsa Craig and Arran, the broadened and still unspoiled lower reaches of the Firth of Clyde, and its main street of whitewashed hotels and boarding-houses, seems to rebuff these grim associations from its past, laying itself out today to please holidaymakers.

From Ballantrae, the coastal road climbs inland, descending to the shores of Loch Ryan through Glen App. A casualty of the Second World War is the little village of Cairnryan, then a military port and a base for flying boats. Here, too, the parts for the Mulberry

Harbour, so essential to the success of the Normandy landings in 1944, were made. Unfortunately, every effort to find a new use for the port has failed, apart from its fairly recent conversion into a ferry terminal for an independently owned roll-on roll-off ferry service to Larne. Most of the crumbling marine ironmongery from long rows of quays and jetties has now been dismantled for scrap. However, there is hope for the place. Apparently the Romans knew it, calling it Rericonius Sinus, and using the loch waters as shelter for their galleys. Nature recovered it from the Roman wars. So perhaps the village may yet either redevelop its lost charm or attract a new industrial purpose.

Passing round the curve at the head of the loch, through the town of Stranraer, the road winds through several hamlets on its way to Kirkcolm. Kirkcolm's main claim to fame is the exasperated ghost said to haunt Caldenoch Castle, near the west shore of the Rhinns. Not only did it make a practice of seizing old women and immersing them in the nearest piece of water, but it drowned the voices of the various ministers who tried to lay it by the administration of psalms. Eventually, in a night-long contest, a new minister triumphed, causing the ghost to utter the weary words: "Roar awa, McGregor, I can roar nae mair!" A little to the south is the charming village of Leswalt, from which a road leads down to Lochnaw and its castle. From the northern point of the Rhinns, the lighthouse of Corsewall Point, to the Mull of Galloway in the south, the peninsula contains a wide variety of historic and scenic interest. The western coastline consists in part of rugged cliffs. The land itself is green and fertile, relaxing down to sandy bays washed by the sea's edge and continually reflecting the light and shade of an open sky. The remains of earthworks and castles, among them Crummag and Dunman, on the western cliffs, are there to remind us of its pre-Christian occupants. Close to the coast of Ireland, it was also known to many of the early Christian teachers.

The largest village on the west coast is Portpatrick, dominated by a large Victorian hotel on a cliff top. The place lies in a kind of rocky amphitheatre, and although it gives the appearance of being sheltered, the harbour is in fact exposed to the prevailing winds for about eight months of the year. Nevertheless, its proximity to Donaghadee, twenty-one and a half miles over the Irish Sea, led to its establishment as a cross-channel port, and as early as 1662 a weekly mail service was established. The first pier was built in 1774, and throughout the latter part of the eighteenth century there was a considerable trade in cattle and horses. In 1821, John Rennie was commissioned to build an artificial harbour at the then enormous cost of £500,000. For a time a paddle-boat mail service plied to and fro, one of its most famous passengers being the actress Mrs Siddons. However, the almost continual swell rolling into the place and the constant damage this caused to the artificial harbour, led eventually to the abandonment of Portpatrick in favour of Stranraer, after which Portpatrick gradually relaxed into becoming a holiday village. It derives its name from the Irish patron saint who, according to legend, once crossed the channel at a single stride. On another occasion, it is claimed that the people of Glen App cut off his head. Picking it up, the saint walked to the sea, and holding his head in his teeth, swam safely back to Ireland: which sounds very Irish indeed! St Cuthbert is said to have landed near Portpatrick when he arrived with Sabina, his mother. The parish church, now ruined, was built in 1628 with revenues from the suppressed abbey of Saulseat. In the graveyard lie sixty sailors from the ship *Orion*, which ran aground in the tumultuous seas around Portpatrick on 18 June 1850.

There is no road down the west coast from Portpatrick to the Mull. A series of minor roads and tracks finger their way west from the main road between Sandhead and Drummore, ending in places with names that have an Irish ring: Cairngarroch, Garrochtrie, Barncarkrie and Cardryne.

Once, the most delightful of these must have been Port Logan, across the bay from the famous Logan gardens. Its row of cottages, now with empty gaps and some of those broad dormer picture windows so disfiguring throughout Wigtownshire, snuggles behind a raised road, which gives some protection from the elements. The story goes that a laird of Logan caused the road to be raised for the very Scottish reason that he could not bear his dependants to have such a good view, such pleasuring being bad for the moral

fibre of the lower orders. The more resourceful dependants, however, simply added an additional storey to their homes. Port Logan
was the birthplace of John M'Lean, 'Hell Fire Jack', a daring sail-
ing-ship skipper who, in a run from the Antipodes, once brought
home his cargo six weeks ahead of the record-breaking clipper
Cutty Sark.

The M'Doualls were the ancient power in this part of the land.
Their stronghold, Logan Castle, is now a ruin, having given place
to Logan House, where later M'Doualls cultivated a splendid
garden, the mild climate of the south-west encouraging not only
palms but plants from Chile, New Zealand, Mexico and Tibet. It
is open to the public, as is the famous Port Logan fish-pond, where
a M'Douall laird constructed an artificial sea-water larder to keep
himself supplied with a stock of cod. The cod who today experience
a period of captivity know no worse fate than to be fed from the
hands of visitors, and released again to the sea before they are
overtaken by the blindness which affects deep-sea fish too long
confined in shallow waters.

Near the Mull of Galloway is St Medan's Cove. She gave her
name to two former chapels; one here, and another at Kirk-
maiden-in-Fernis, on the shores of Monreith Bay. She is said
miraculously to have made the crossing from west to east on a
floating rock minus her eyesight, having torn out her eyes to re-
pulse an over-ardent lover. At Monreith, water from a spring
restored her damaged vision. Near St Medan's Cove is the well of
the Co'. On the first Sunday in May, known as Co' Sunday, the
people of Drummore came here to bathe in the well, which was
credited with remarkable medicinal properties. Coins from reigns
as far back as Charles I have been uncovered, doubtless left behind
with thanks for services miraculously rendered.

There are those who believe with Stevenson that:

> From the bonnie bells of heather
> They brewed a drink long-syne,
> Was sweeter far than honey,
> Was stronger far than wine.

Heather ale was supposed to be a Pictish speciality. The last
Pictish chief to defend the Double Dykes, said to be the scene of

the final defence of the Picts against the invading Scots from Ireland, took the secret with him. A treacherous Druid, having revealed that the secret was known only to the chief and his two sons, brought about a confrontation. One son promised to tell the invaders the secret of the brew if his father and brother were first flung over the cliffs so that they could not witness his treachery. There was no difficulty in meeting this requirement. The survivor, however, then immediately threw himself after his relatives, shouting, "The secret dies".

The lighthouse, built in 1828, stands sixty feet high, beyond the Double Dykes, on the Mull's headland, a great paw raised against the sea. On a clear day it is possible to see the Isle of Man, twenty-two miles away, and Ireland, twenty-six miles distant.

Drummore, the southernmost village in Scotland, looks across to Port William, on the other side of Luce Bay, and up the bay itself. It is now mainly a sleepy holiday village with a tidal harbour, although once it was a small port, exporting coal and lime. Its castle ceased to be lived in at the end of the seventeenth century. Inland from Sandhead, the church of Kirkmadrine possesses in its porch two stones thought to be the oldest Christian monuments in Scotland. Their inscriptions commemorate in Roman capitals three bishops or priests, and were probably carved in the fifth century, not long after the end of the Roman occupation and the death of St Ninian.

Stonykirk, on the overland road from Luce Bay to Loch Ryan, was the scene of a highly original murder. A seventeenth-century laird of Balgreggan disliked his minister, the Reverend Robert Campbell, so gave him poisoned wine. By the time the poor minister took his homeward way, he was already starting to swell. He dropped dead near the village, and was then propped up with his walking stick against the dyke by villagers, who presumably either shared the laird's extreme dislike of his sermons, or carelessly assumed that their minister was merely drunk.

On a bank of the Water of Luce, overlooking Luce Bay, is the abbey of Glenluce, founded in 1190 by Roland, Lord of Galloway, and now in the care of the Scottish Development Department. It has associations with the thirteenth-century wizard Michael Scott.

He managed to persuade some witches, whose attentions had become inconvenient, to pass their time spinning ropes from the sands of Luce Bay. By the seventeenth century, however, supernatural cures took longer. Four years elapsed before the local Presbytery could placate the devil of Glenluce, who haunted Gilbert Campbell from 1654 to 1658. Though trembled by constant traffic and scarred by thoughtless developments and modernizations, the hillside village of Glenluce still has considerable charm. Two miles north-east is Carscreugh Castle, a Stair house. The enforced betrothal of Lord Stair's daughter, Janet, gave Scott the theme of *The Bride of Lammermoor*. Five miles up the Water of Luce is the village of New Luce, where 'Prophet' Alexander Peden preached from 1659 till 1662, before taking to the hills.

The rather dour little town of Whithorn—mentioned by Ptolemy, in the second century, as the Leukopibia of the Novantae tribe, a Greek corruption synonymous with the Latin Candida Casa or White House—has the site of a priory much visited by royal and other pilgrims. The charming seaside village of Isle of Whithorn is now stranded on nothing more severing than a peninsula. Its trade with Whitehaven and other English ports has long since vanished, leaving its little harbour, constructed in 1790, entirely given over to the bobbing boats of holidaymakers. It has the remains of a Scandinavian camp and the roofless ruin of St Ninian's Kirk, once wrongly believed to be the Candida Casa of A.D. 397, though the real chapel was probably associated with Whithorn Priory. Isle of Whithorn is now a conservation area, as is the badly gapped Garlieston, further up the coast. It, too, is made up of little more than a couple of streets behind a crescent of houses fronting a bay, its boat-building, fishing, manufacture of chemicals and its export and import trade all things of the past. It was founded two hundred years ago by Lord Garlies, who later became John, seventh Earl of Galloway. It stands near Galloway House, until recently the family home of the Galloways.

Through the towns of Wigtown and Newton Stewart, over the River Cree, through Minnigaff, down the eastern coast of Wigtown Bay and past the hamlets of Palnure and Spittal, the inland village of Creetown is reached, the Port-an-Ferry of Scott's *Guy Manner-*

ing. Creetown granite built not only most of the village, including
the hideous tower clock erected to mark Queen Victoria's Diamond
Jubilee—Galloway possesses several of these oddities—but also
the Thames Embankment and the Mersey docks. Between Cree-
town and Gatehouse of Fleet—the road allegedly said by Thomas
Carlyle, in response to a question from Queen Victoria, to be the
finest road in the kingdom, the next finest being the road from
Gatehouse of Fleet to Creetown—it is not so much the village
but the wider natural prospects that delight. The road leads past
Carsluith Castle, birthplace of the last abbot of Sweetheart Abbey,
Dick Hatteraick's Cave, and, with but a slight deviation, Barholm
Castle and grim Cardoness, the latter once the home of the Galloway MacCullochs and the Gordons of Lochinvar. It is worth making
an additional small diversion to look at Anwoth, just outside Gatehouse. Within the ivy-covered roofless ruined church the Gordons
are buried, the verses on some of the tombstones wearing a look of
surprising distinction, but plagiarized by some mortuary poetaster
from Glasgow Cathedral and elsewhere. This was the church of the
word-struck Samuel Rutherford, the mixed metaphors of whose
letters and sermons keep them among the curiosities of seventeenth-century Scottish prose. His manse was taken down when
the present church was being built. Again we are reminded that we
are in what was strong Covenanting country, for the graveyard
contains the earthly remains of John Bell of Whiteside, executed
for his beliefs by Grier of Lag.

One effect of the development of rail and, later, of road traffic,
was the inevitable strangulation from behind of countless little
village and small town ports. One of these was Gatehouse of Fleet,
originally a linear village laid out by William Murray. It was for
him that nearby Cally House was built in 1763 to plans by Robert
Milne. A vast portico with huge granite pillars was added by
Papworth in 1830. The house is now an hotel, the estate a state
forest, and the village, intended to be an industrial town, largely
residential and a centre for tourists. In its brief industrial heyday,
it achieved half-a-dozen cotton mills, a brewery, a tannery, and
even a shipbuilding yard. Lord Cockburn, that vivid recorder of
traveller's impressions, described it as "too visibly the village at

the Great Man's gate". The family no longer own Cally House, but still have influence in the village, an influence that, in pre-conservation area days, undoubtedly prevented its despoliation.

The main road winds its way inland, crossing the River Dee into Kirkcudbright. From this delightful town the A762 leads north to New Galloway, passing the shores of Loch Ken and joining up with the A712. This goes out from Newton Stewart to New Galloway, past Clatteringshaws Loch, giving splendid prospects of the hill Cairnsmore of Fleet and the Cairn Edward Forest by Glen Trool. New Galloway is a hilly linear village and a royal burgh holding its charter from Charles I. Its white houses, some of them edged with black-painted corner stones, and its profusion of trees, give it an unforgettable setting, particularly in early summer when the boughs hang rich with coloured blossom. Less than a mile away is the sixteenth-century Kenmure Castle. Its owner, Sir John Gordon, loyally supported Mary, Queen of Scots. His grandson, also Sir John, was created Viscount Kenmure by Charles I. William, the sixth Viscount—the hero of Burns's splendid song "Kenmure's up and awa"—was 'out' at the 1715 rising, got himself caught and was subsequently beheaded on London's Tower Hill.

The A712 twists its way eastward, through magnificent country to Dumfries. Back on the coast road, however, we find ourselves in Dundrennan, its twelfth-century abbey now a sadly quarried ruin, still lending solemn distinction to the little village built from its plundered stones. In a wall recess there is a fifteenth-century carved slab to the memory of Sir William Livingstoun of Culter, who died in 1607, and another to a fighting abbot and his mur-derer, the murderer's dagger engraved in the abbot's heart, the pastoral crook piercing the head of the murderer. Mary, Queen of Scots is supposed to have spent her last night in Scotland in or near Dundrennan Abbey. On the morning of 16 May 1568 she left Scotland for ever, probably from either Abbey Burnfoot or Port Mary, two of the tidal creeks so numerous along the Solway Coast.

Auchencairn, a village on a hillside, looks out across the bay from which it takes its name. Heston Isle, a feature of the bay, is the Isle Rathan of S. R. Crockett's novel *The Raiders*. The walk to Balcary Point passes Balcary House, a strongly cellared edifice built by a combine of smugglers. Before reaching Palnackie, it is worth making a diversion to Orchardton, which possesses the only free-standing round tower in Scotland. It was built in the fifteenth century by John Cairns, and eventually came into the hands of the Maxwells, the ending of whose line provided Scott with the theme of *Guy Mannering*. At Palnackie, on the Urr Water, the river broadens into the Rough Firth. Round it are charming places of twentieth-century pleasure; residential Rockcliffe and marine-minded Kippford, as well as rocks and caves with names like Brandy Cave, the Piper's Cove and the Murderer's Well.

Continuing round the coast road, and making a diversion via the coast to Southernness, a holiday-home settlement with a striking eighteenth-century lighthouse, the inland village of Kirkbean is reached. In this lush green country the sea is never far away. In 1747, at Arbigland, on the coast near Kirkbean, a certain John Paul was born in a gamekeeper's cottage. The young man went to sea at seventeen aboard a slave transport, and eventually settled in America, assuming the surname Jones after the American family who had befriended him. In 1775 he was given a commission in the American Navy, whose official founder he became. In the American war against Britain, he raided the east and west coasts, striking at places as far apart as Whitehaven and Arbroath, and with typical English provincialism was promptly dubbed a pirate. In 1945 a baptismal font was presented to Kirkbean Church by the officers and men of the United States Navy who served in Great Britain during the War. It acknowledges Jones as the first commander of the United States Navy. Piracy was no longer mentioned. On one of the panels it commemorates the *Bonhomme Richard*, the ship from which Jones fought his famous battle off Flamborough Head.

Up the coast, Carsethorn's Steamboat Inn is a relic of the days when the Liverpool steam packet regularly called here, and the villages and hamlets of the treacherous Solway estuary were still dependent on the skills of mariners for their supplies.

The tiny conservation area village of New Abbey, at the foot of Criffel, takes its name from Sweetheart or New Abbey, the Cistercian abbey dedicated to the Virgin founded in 1275 by Devorguilla, who also founded Balliol College, Oxford and built the old bridge at Dumfries. Third daughter of Allan, Lord of Galloway, and a great-great-granddaughter of David I, she was mother of the vassal king, John Balliol. Her own husband, John de Balliol, died in 1269 at Barnard Castle. Devorguilla had his heart embalmed and casketted, to be laid in due time upon her own when she was buried before the high altar at New Abbey, thus *Dulce Cor* became Sweetheart Abbey. The tracery of the west rose-window, the east window and those of choir, clerestory and north transept are entire and beautiful. The abbey merges Early English style with the beginnings of Second Pointed or Decorated style, and so in a sense is transitional. Its last abbot, Gilbert Brown of Carsluith, became the prototype of the main character in Scott's novel *The Abbot*.

On the road from New Galloway to Castle Douglas, down the east coast of Loch Ken, the hamlet of Parton has the remains of a sixteenth-century church, now used as a burial vault. Its carved pulpit, dated 1598, is in Edinburgh's Museum of Antiquities. Crossmichael is named after St Michael, its annual festival being the Michaelmas Fair. The cross round which the fair was held has long since disappeared, but the grave of its martyr, William Graham, shot by a party of Claverhouse's troops in 1682, remains. On a minor road between the A745 and the A712, Kirkpatrick-Durham looks over pleasant pastoral country from the edge of a moor. It has preserved its early nineteenth-century appearance and the memory of six Covenanters, shot on a March day in 1685 by one Captain Bruce, and commemorated in sincere but execrable verse. Haugh of Urr has a bridge over the Urr Water built in 1760. A mile and a half further down the river is the Mote of Urr, with the outlined remains of a fortification of the mote and bailey type. One of Galloway's most attractive features are its peaceful hamlets like Milton of Urr, having no particular history; fleeting pleasures to the traveller in one of the most beautiful and still least explored areas of Scotland whose richest heritage is natural rather than man-made.

Of the villages along the coast between Dumfries and Gretna, Glencaple, on the Nith Estuary, and once the stopping place for larger ships unable to get up to Dumfries, was founded in 1747.

With its delightful view across the Nith to Criffel, it is now not so much a seaside resort as a centre for the sailing of small craft. Near the mouth of the Nith stands Caerlaverock Castle, begun near the end of the fourteenth century, although an earlier castle at or near the same site preceded it. It provided a base for the Lords Maxwell, its proprietors, to raid the north of England during the second half of the fifteenth century. James V was staying there at the time of the rout of the Scots at Solway Moss in 1542. The English under the Earl of Sussex besieged it and took it in 1570, partially destroying it. The first Earl of Nithsdale repaired it in 1638, adding its present Renaissance features. Sadly, after it ceased to be lived in at the end of the seventeenth century, it fell gradually into ruin.

The otherwise unnoteworthy hamlet of Ruthwell, near Brow, where Burns was sent to sea-bathe so disastrously in the last months of his life, is distinguished because it possesses the Ruthwell Cross, a runic monument nearly eighteen feet high. Until a few decades ago, it stood in the churchyard, but has now been removed for protection to a sunken well inside the little church. On one of its faces are carved verses from Caedmon's lay of *The Holy Rood*. It is thought that the cross was set up around A.D. 680 at Priestside, near the sea, and drawn to the parish church by a team of oxen. In 1642, however, it was overthrown and broken in pieces, one of which turned up on an eighteenth-century grave. The whole thing was re-erected in 1802 by the Reverend Henry Duncan, minister from 1799 until the Disruption. Incidentally, it was this same Dr Duncan who in 1810 established at Ruthwell the earliest savings bank in Scotland.

Cummertrees was designed as a major watering-place, but failed to develop. Its English-style vaguely mock-Tudor Edwardian suburban houses must strike the golfer *en route* for Powfoot as strange in their context.

In the rich hinterland, threaded by a maze of backroads, pleasant little agricultural villages like Mouswald, Dalton, Torthorwald, Hightae and Bridekirk are come upon. The most important of these landward places is Ecclefechan, now by-passed by the Carlisle–Glasgow road. Here, Thomas Carlyle was born in 1795. The red sandstone of the district gives the houses a sober glow, which contrasts with those traditionally whitewashed. Carlyle's father and uncle are supposed to have been connected with the building of the original village. Carlyle's house is now a museum, in the care of The National Trust for Scotland. The 'Sage of Chelsea' was buried in the churchyard on 10 February 1881, in a cemetery which also contains the remains of Dr Archibald Arnott, Napoleon's doctor at St Helena.

The A74 Carlisle to Glasgow road now by-passes all the hamlets on the route; even Beattock, which grew up around the railway station in 1803 to serve the little town of Moffat, where rich people who fancied themselves ill went to drink goatsmilk in earlier days and in Victorian times the more expensive waters of the hydropathic.

On the A76, from Dumfries to Kilmarnock, a little to the north of the pleasant small agricultural town of Thornhill, is Carronbridge, one of Dumfriesshire's conservation areas. It lies in a dip and on a curve, where the A702 road over the Lowther Hills from Crawford joins the A76, and crosses the Carron Water shortly before it merges with the Nith. This road resumes its identity in Thornhill itself, striking west to St John's Town of Dalry, in Galloway, and passing the villages of Penpont and Moniaive. Moniaive, a delightful village set in land between the Dalwhat and Craigdarrock Waters, became a burgh of barony under charter from Charles I. Nearby is the house of Maxwelton, once the home of the Laurie family and so lived in by Annie, the heroine of the popular Scottish song. During the 1960s it became the home of the late Hugh Stenhouse, who, with his wife, took down the Victorian accretions and restored the older house, a model of good taste and impeccable contemporary craftsmanship.

Further up the Nith valley, on the left bank of Kirk Burn, is Durisdeer, another conservation area and a village both beautiful and full of historical interest. Dorothy Wordsworth, who saw this countryside with Coleridge and her brother when driving from Thornhill to Wanlockhead in August 1804, described how they stopped their jaunting car, and walked: "into a field where we looked down upon the Nith, which runs far below on a deep and rocky channel; the banks woody; the view pleasant down the river to Thornhill; an open country, corn fields, pastures, and scattered trees." The village is an unspoilt group of agricultural cottages, many of them listed, an old mill once visited by Burns, and a cruciform church, possibly designed by Sir William Bruce and built in 1699. In the northern transept is the Queensberry Mausoleum. Two sculptured figures after the manner of Roubilliac, imported from Rome, represent James, the second Duke of Queensberry, who died in 1711, and his duchess. Nearby is the Enterkin Pass of which Dr John Brown, the Victorian author of *Horae Subsecivae*, wrote:

a few steps and you are on its edge, looking down giddy and amazed into its sudden and immense depths. . . . We know nothing more noticeable, more unlike any other place, more impressive, than this short, deep, narrow and sudden glen. There is only room for its own stream at the bottom, and the sides rise in one smooth and all but perpendicular ascent to the height, on the left, of 1,895 feet in Thirstane Hill, and on the right, of 1,875 feet in the exquisitely moulded Steygail, or Steep Gable, so steep that it is no easy matter keeping your feet. . . .

In his *Memoirs of the Church of Scotland in Four Periods* (1717) Daniel Defoe describes the rescue in the Pass by a party under James and Thomas Harkness of a minister and five Covenanters being taken as prisoners to Edinburgh in July 1684.

Dalton is a typical south of Scotland early nineteenth-century agricultural village, many of its homes listed and with a parish church dating from 1704. Tinwald has a church built in 1763, Tinwaldshaws, a 'big hoose', put up in 1751, and Robert Adam's Tinwald House itself, mid-eighteenth century but with a reconstructed interior following a fire in 1946.

In Eskdale parish, apart from the bleak little village of Eskdalemuir itself, where an observatory is located, the most interesting village is Canonbie. It stands on the left bank of the Esk, here an impressive river well on its way to merge with the Solway. Canonbie's quality is its group value, set in a particularly picturesque valley. The parish church dates from 1822.

5

Fife and Kinross

EVER since that versifying chronicler Andrew of Wyntoun described Fife as a 'Kynrick' or Kingdom, so it has been known. With
the Forth and Tay estuaries washing its flanks, and Loch Leven and
the Lomond Hills backing it, it has preserved its sense of identity
for centuries; an identity which was to force the late twentieth-
century's reformers of local government to abandon their intention
of splitting it in two, by estuarial allegiance. Once, the town of
Dunfermline had both a royal palace and an abbey. Later, Falkland
was a royal residence. And when Christianity abandoned its Celtic
customs in favour of Roman ones, it was not long before Iona gave
place to St Andrews as Scotland's Christian centre.

In Stuart times, the little fishing towns along the East Neuk
carried on trade with the Low Countries and the Hanseatic ports,
from their trim harbours lined with red-pantiled vernacular houses.
The broad Howe of Fife was, then, as it still is, the granary of
the kingdom. Coal-mining, carried on locally by medieval monks,
was to transform completely the southern part of Fife during the
nineteenth century.

The traveller in search of Fife's most interesting villages is not
likely to spend too much time in industrialized southern Fife, although if he arrives over the Kincardine Bridge, it would be worth
his while to take a look at the high street of Kincardine-on-Forth.
The mercat cross is a Corinthian pillar which carries on its capital
the arms of the Earls of Kincardine. Tradition has it that the Earl
of Elgin and Kincardine has the right to drive a coach and four
round the mercat cross, a right, however, not recently exercised.

The very Scots-looking Tulliallan Parish Church, now ruined, dates from the seventeenth century, having been superseded by a Gothic Revival building of 1819.

Kincardine was once an important port, where small ships were built. It was the birthplace in 1842 of Sir James Dewar, the inventor of the vacuum flask. Near the town are the ruins of Tulliallan Castle, once a Blackadder stronghold inhabited from the twelfth to the latter part of the seventeenth centuries, and a paper mill on the site of Kilbagie Distillery, celebrated by Burns in "The Jolly Beggars".

A little along the coast lies Culross. By the accident of chance, it has survived to be preserved in our own day as a splendid example of a small Scottish burgh of the sixteenth and seventeenth centuries. Most of the little houses in Culross have beeen restored by The National Trust for Scotland. So has Bishop Leighton's house known as The Study, and the palace of the coal-owning Sir George Bruce of Carnock. Inside the palace there are splendid painted barrel ceilings and seventeenth-century decorative mural work.

James VI visited Sir George's colliery in 1617. Unaware that the workings passed under the Forth, when led up one of the shafts that opened out upon an island in mid-channel, he immediately yelled "Treason!", and had to be reassured that the boat which stood by merely waited to carry him back to the shore.

Culross still possesses its original mercat cross. Its abbey stands at the top of Tanhouse Brae, looking over the Forth. A religious building is thought to have occupied this ground since the time of the fifth-century St Serf. A monastery was founded by Malcolm, sixth Earl of Fife, in 1217, for the White Monks of the Cistercian Order. The appropriately named Abbot Andrew Masoun was responsible for the building of the four-storeyed tower about 1500. Another abbot, James Inglis, one of the poets of the age now scarcely remembered, was murdered in 1531 by John Blackadder of Tulliallan, aided in the deed by a monk, William Louthian, both of whom were duly beheaded. The Culross Psalter, now in Edinburgh's Advocates' Library, is an example of the fine manuscript work carried out by this community.

G

The present church has been much rebuilt, although the arch-
ways to the south transept date from about 1300 and the existing
windows from the fifteenth century. In the north transept is the
Argyll tomb, the Argylls of Castle Campbell, near Dollar, having
been overlords of Culross Abbey. There is also the tomb of Sir
George Bruce and his wife, ancestors of the Earls of Elgin and
Kincardine. Another interesting tomb is that of one of the de
Quencis, thought to have died towards the end of the thirteenth
century.

In the second storey of the tower there is a witches' chamber,
used for the imprisonment of these unfortunate women when the
Tolbooth was full. The bells and clock in the third storey date from
the seventeenth century.

Next to the abbey grounds are the ruins of Culross Abbey House,
built in 1608 but demolished in 1830 to make way for a later
structure. Dunimarle Castle, a nineteenth-century imitation fortalice, is said to occupy the site of an earlier castle in which Lady
Macduff and her children were murdered.

No one could nowadays claim independent village status for
North Queensferry, Aberdour—though it still has a ruined castle
and its old harbour, from which it is possible to sail to Inchcolm
—or even Kinghorn, let alone Kirkcaldy, Dysart or Leven. The old
part of Inverkeithing, however, is a conservation area, as is the
heart of West Wemyss which has a much altered seventeenth-
century church and a good town steeple. But before proceeding
further up the Fife coast, let us retrace our steps to take in what
has been by-passed.

Auchtertool, at the end of Puddledub Road, off the A907 from
Dunfermline to Kirkcaldy, has wide sweeping views along its
approaches. Sir James Kirkcaldy's mansion of Hallyards once
stood here. James V, after his defeat at Solway Moss, rested a
night there on his way back to Falkland. William Sinclair,
Bishop of Dunkeld, backed by some sixty ill-equipped retainers,
sallied forth from Auchtertool in 1317 to throw back a detachment of Edward II's troops that had advanced on Dunfermline.
Near Auchtertool are the ruins of Knockdavie Castle, once owned
by a member of the Douglas family and a persecutor of the Cov-

enanters. Balmuto Tower, its fourteenth-century stones now built into a modern house, is also nearby.

Travelling north through Lochgelly, a development of the growth of mining, the old village of Auchterderran has only its eighteenth-century church as a reminder of its rural past. The winning of coal, like the establishment and operation of the industries necessary to enable us to keep our place in the world, has extracted a high environmental price. This was particularly true in the nineteenth century. However much it is possible to minimize environmental havoc from mining today by exercising stricter controls than in the past, a price will constantly have to be paid. This, perhaps, is an appropriate reflection for those travelling through the Fife coalfields, with their sense of uniform utilitarian drabness.

Now and then, though, there are surprises, like the village of Kinglassie, a cluster of red pantile-roofed cottages by a burn in a hollow. Ballingry, reputedly established by monks sent from Loch Leven by St Serf, has a church which, though rebuilt in 1831, still contains much of its older fabric. The church is mentioned in Scott's novel *The Abbot*. From nearby Lochore, Sir Walter's son took his wife, Jane Jobson, the daughter of a wealthy industrialist.

Falkland is dominated by its royal palace, though a palace closely linked to the vernacular houses of the retainers who once served it. In the grounds of the palace are the remains of the tower of Falkland, where the Duke of Albany is supposed to have been responsible for the death by starvation of the twenty-year-old son of Robert III, the Duke of Rothesay. In point of fact a Parliamentary Inquiry at the time exonerated Albany and his colleague Douglas of murder, though the suspicion remained strong enough to become "bydand legend" and inspire Scott's novel *The Fair Maid of Perth*. The palace came to James I when the Earldom of Fife was forfeited. James II, James III and James IV all added to its fabric. In it James IV entertained Perkin Warbeck and his cousin, Lady Catherine Gordon, who became Warbeck's wife. The imprisoned James V escaped to Stirling from the palace, which was by then much dilapidated. James V later turned to restoring it as a residence worthy of himself and his queen. The notorious Sir James Hamilton of Finnart, executed for treason in 1540, was in charge of the restoration, but the work was completed by John Scrymgeour of the Myres.

Inside may be seen the black oak bed on which James V is supposed to have died, turning his face to the wall when he learned that at Linlithgow it was a princess and not a son and heir that his wife had borne. "It cam wi' a lass an it'll gang wi' a lass!" were his famous last words. There are fine portraits of James V and his queen, as well as of James V as a young man, Anne of Denmark, Prince Henry and Charles II. The third Marquis of Bute, kinsman of the Crichton–Stuart hereditary keepers of the palace, did much to forward the restoration of Falkland begun by the Bruces of Falkland in 1823. The Bute restorations, carried out after the marquis had acquired it in 1888, included the refurbishing of the Royal Chapel, which still has its King's pew and original pulpit, though the seventeenth-century Flemish tapestries on the chapel walls are later acquisitions.

Mary, James V's "lass", visited Falkland soon after her marriage to Darnley, and again after the birth of her own son. Falkland became his favourite residence. It was here, in 1596, when a commission from the General Assembly, then at Cupar, paid a visit, that the exasperated James VI, listening unwillingly to James Melville, interrupted so often that one of their number, Andrew Melville, called him "God's silly vassal", adding: "Now again I maun tell you there is twa kings in Scotland. Thair is Christ Jesus the King, and His Kingdom and Kirk, whose subject King James the Saxth is, and of whose Kingdom not a king, nor a lord, nor a heid, but a member". In spite of this rankling memory, James VI took the time to visit it just before making his royal progress south in 1603.

Sir David Lyndsay, who was attached to the court of both James IV and James V, spent much time at this royal palace, and although he complained about the badness of the local beer, he enjoyed himself enough to celebrate his stay in verse:

> Fare weill, Falkland, the fortress of Fyfe,
>   Thy polite park, under the Lowmound Law,
> Sum tyme in thee I led a lustie lyfe.
>   The fallow deer, to see thame raik on raw,

Court men to cum to thee thay stand grait awe,
Sayand, they burgh bene of all burrowis haill,
Because, in thee, they never gat guid ale.

During the abortive Jacobite Rising of 1715, Rob Roy and his followers, who had marched to Sheriffmuir without actually taking part in the battle, moved to Falkland, seized the village and levied compulsory 'contributions' from the inhabitants.

Falkland House, built around 1840 for the Marquis of Bute by William Burn, stands just under three-quarters of a mile west of the town.

One of Fife's surprisingly few rural conservation areas, Falkland still has many fine vernacular houses, a gracious Town House built in 1802, the homes of Nicol Moncrieff, dated 1610, and the neighbouring residence of the Royal Falconer, dated 1607. On the south side of Parliament Square is the birthplace of Richard Cameron, schoolmaster of Falkland. It is now a shop, though marked with a plaque. Born in 1648, Cameron, a staunch Covenanter, was nicknamed the 'Lion of the Covenant'. The founder of the Cameronian regiment, he was killed at Airds Moss.

Falkland once had an odd distinction. In 1781, water was brought from the nearby Lomond Hills by pipes for storing in wells. For the times, the place had thus one of the finest water supplies in Scotland. The Gothic-style church, built in 1849, was a gift from the strangely named Onesiphorous Tyndall-Bruce, an Englishman who married Miss Bruce of Falkland. For his financial contribution towards the restoration of the palace he is commemorated by a statue nearby.

To the east of Falkland lie the neat little villages of Kingskettle, Freuchie and Ladybank. Kingskettle was originally called Cautel, or Katul, an ancient word for 'battle'. Kingskettle's Gothic church dates from 1831, the third in the parish that has served the village. The first, at Lathrisk, came into use in 1243. The remains of its vestry are built into the outer kitchen of Lathrisk House. The vestry of the second church, closed in 1636, does duty as a garden tool-shed. Linen was once manufactured at Kingskettle—the use of the royal 'King's' was granted by a charter of 1541—though now it is simply a peaceful agricultural village. Freuchie, a winding village of quaint charm, also once possessed linen factories. More anciently, it is said to be the place where disgraced courtiers were sent to meditate upon their offending indiscretions, hence, perhaps, the saying 'Awa tae Freuchie and fry mice", although possibly the mice bit is a twentieth-century addition! Ladybank, deriving its name from 'Our Lady's Bog', was originally a peat moss granted to the monks of Lindores to supply the abbey with fuel, and so named by them. It was at one time a busier railway junction when Fife was more plentifully served with train services than it is now. It still has one of the best listed railway stations of the 1840s.

Gateside stands at the entrance to the Howe of Fife. The remains of a Roman camp and the discovery of several pits containing skulls suggest that a considerable battle must have taken place in the vicinity. Most authorities do not agree with the local tradition that this was the site of the Battle of Mons Graupius, in which the Scots army was led by Calgacus; a battle for the actuality of which we have the report of Tacitus.

Lying to the north-west, Strathmiglo also had links with Falkland. In the sixteenth century, Sir William Scott of Balwearie had the lands of Cairne, formerly Wester Strathmiglo, conferred on him by James VI. Wanting to be near the court at Falkland, he built himself Strathmiglo Castle, which his sovereign ungraciously nicknamed 'Cairnie-Flappet'. By 1734 the castle was in ruins, its stones being used by the locals to build their town houses. The tower carries the arms of the Balfours of Burleigh, who took over the lands of Strathmiglo from the Scotts of Balwearie about 1600. The stone sundial below their arms came from the village cross. Strathmiglo's former religious associations are perpetuated in the district names, Kirklands, on the south side of the principal street, and Templelands, on the same side nearer the middle of the place. The main street runs parallel to the River Eden, formerly the Miglo. The handsome steeple, seventy feet high, has an open balustrade and an octagonal spire.

Passing Dunshelt, until a hundred years or so ago known as Daneshalt because it was thought that at this place the Danes halted when they fled from a defeat on Falkland Moor, we reach

Auchtermuchty, now arguably a small town rather than a large village. Until 1960 it used to be famous for its thatched roofs, thatching being the common method of roofing in the Howe of Fife. For many years the rushes came from the banks of the Tay near Newburgh. The name is said to derive from the Gaelic *uachdar-nuic*, 'the upper land of the wild sow'. It became a royal burgh in 1517 and provided the setting for one of the most famous old Scots poems that tells of a wife and a husband who each thinks the other works less hard, "The Wife of Auchtermuchty", at one time wrongly attributed to James V. In 1816 the burgh went bankrupt, and all its corporation property was sequestered with the exception of the Town House, the jail, the steeple and the bell. In 1950 when a clapper fell from the bell during Sunday service, it was discovered that it was a silver pre-Reformation bell, probably one of the four bells from Lindores Abbey lost when Lindores was overrun by the Reformers. The pleasing bridges over the Muchtie Burn allegedly once led James V to advise someone who had spoken well of London's bridges to "ride round the Howe. There in my Royal Burgh of Auchtermuchtie you will find bridges more worthy of note than that which spans the Thames!" The Reverend John Glas (1698–1773), who founded the sect of Glasites, was born in the place. Nearby Myres Castle was once the home of the Moncrieffs of Reddie.

Moving north from Falkland, or east from Auchtermuchty, the village of Collessie is reached. Rossie Loch, which once lay beside it, was drained in 1740. It was by the shores of this loch that King James V, wandering about in the guise of "the Gude Man o' Ballangeich", is supposed to have encouraged a shepherd and asked him, pointing towards Falkland, "Wha stays in that muckle house?" "They ca' him the king," the shepherd answered, "but we ca' him the Guid Man. They say he makes a lot o' dirty knichts."

While the shepherd's attention was diverted, the king pocketed an awl with which the man had been mending shoes. When he noticed the awl gone, the shepherd accused the stranger of having stolen it. In the middle of the ensuing argument, some of the king's knights rode up and made obeisance to him. The shepherd realized that he had accused his king of theft. He was ordered to strip and wade into the muddy loch as a punishment. When he came ashore, mud-covered, the king created him a knight, with the comment: "Of a' the dirty knights I've made, I never made a dirtier."

Stories of this sort, however apocryphal, are unlikely to gather round unpleasant monarchs. Their literary inspiration is possibly the once widely popular old Scots poem "Rauf Collyear".

There are interesting pre-historic monuments in the area, none more so than Gask Hill, excavated in 1876, when it was found to contain a Bronze Age skeleton, some decorated urns and a Bronze dagger blade. Sir James Melville (1535–1607) held the nearby estate of Hallhill. His *Memoirs*, describing his ambassadorial services on behalf of Mary, Queen of Scots, make fascinating reading and have been frequently republished since his death. In the former parish church, Burns's Edinburgh friend Dr Hugh Blair (1718–1800), began his ministry. The present building dates from 1829.

Two miles south-east of Newburgh is the village of Lindores. At the end of the eighteenth century, the remains of a castle, believed to be that of Macduff, Thane of Fife, were uncovered. Built into a wall at the other end of the village is an old stone with carving on it thought to have had some religious significance in sun-worshipping times. The Loch of Lindores lies a little away from the village road, but in the grounds of Abdie Church the ruins of the pre-Reformation church of St Magridin still survive. This was the site of a Culdee settlement, and the church was dedicated in 1242 by the Bishop of St Andrews, David de Berham, remaining in use until 1827. In the aisle there are monuments to the Balfours of Denmilne, and in the churchyard, the grave of Rear-Admiral Frederick Lewis Maitland, whose home was at Lindores House. He was a founder of the Caledonian Curling Club. His main claim to fame, however, was that it was he who received Napoleon on board the *Bellerophon* after his defeat at Waterloo.

Lindores Abbey, standing in a fertile hollow near the Tay, has a site of such great beauty that it is impossible not to regret its destruction at the hands of Knox and his followers in 1559, when they overthrew the altars and statues and burned the Mass books.

Now that the majority of the population of Scotland are no longer practising supporters of the religion instituted by Knox, at the cost of the destruction of so much of our architectural heritage, one may surely be pardoned for wondering if the Presbyterian faith—or any other, for that matter—was really worth the human and artistic cost! To a twentieth-century humanist it must always seem strange that a supposedly omnipotent God should be unduly concerned about the precise sectarian forms used for His worship!

Be that as it may, the abbey, as may still be seen from its extensive ruins, must have been mightily imposing. It was founded in 1178 by David, Earl of Huntingdon, for the Benedictine Order, and laid out in sacred earth specially brought from Ireland. John Leslie, the last Abbot of Lindores, was a warm supporter of Mary, Queen of Scots. After his death, the revenues from its lands fell to Sir Patrick Leslie, who was created the first Lord Lindores. Incredible as it may seem, it was then that the real work of destruction of the fabric began, the stones being used as a quarry for domestic buildings. During its 400 years of active existence, Edward I descended to force the leaders of the three Estates to accept him as their Liege Lord. It was on this trip that he annexed the Coronation Stone from Scone, in Perthshire. Here, too, Sir William Wallace celebrated his victory over the English at the nearby battlefield of Earnside. Beneath the rugged crag of Clachard, that geographically must once have tied the northern fringe of Fife to the Grampians across the Tay, stands Newburgh. It is really a town now, and so falls outwith our survey. However, its development was closely tied to that of Lindores Abbey, and its ancient privileges were upheld by charters from the abbot. The Cross of Mugdrum, with its Celtic patterned decorations, is worth visiting, as is Macduff's Cross, which inspired Scott to write his poem of that name.

Between Newburgh and Cupar, which lies at the centre of north Fife, one or two villages should be noted. Monimail, with its beeches, its yews and its well ordered gardens once served Monimail Palace, which belonged to the Archbishop of St Andrews. The last Roman Catholic Archbishop of St Andrews, Archbishop Hamilton, while living there was cured of an illness, probably asthma, by an Italian astrologer, Cardan, brought to Scotland at the archbishop's invitation. The water used in the cure—about which successful medicos wrote a profitable book—came from a spring known as Cardan's Well. However, the unfortunate archbishop, who tried unsuccessfully to persuade Mary, Queen of Scots, from entrusting herself to Elizabeth, was captured at Dumbarton Castle wearing armour underneath his cassock in April 1571, and soon afterwards was hanged at Stirling Castle.

There are strong literary associations with this part of Fife. The Mount was the site of the home of the poet Sir David Lyndsay (1498–1555), author of *Ane Satyre of the Thrie Estatis*, the morality play revived in our own day with great success at Edinburgh International Festival. On the summit of Mount Hill is a Doric column in memory of John, fourth Earl of Hopetoun (1766–1823), a hero of the Peninsular Wars. Sir Robert Sibbald (1641–1712), the doctor and antiquary whose memoirs still make interesting reading, was born in Monimail and made his home in Upper Rankeillour. The two 'Peasant Poets', Alexander Bethune (1804–43) and his brother John (1802–39), were also born in Monimail, but after their early deaths were buried in Abdie Churchyard, Lindores. They are more or less forgotten now, but John's understandably radical sentiments are still occasionally quoted:

> Rejoice! And why?—To live unseen,
> An object of neglect.
> And see the vain, the vile, the mean,
> Surrounded with respect;
> To be in life's loud bustle lost,
> And look on creeping things
> With nothing save their wealth to boast,
> Worshipped as Lords and Kings.

Melville House was built in 1697 for the first Earl of Melville, by James Smith. It is one of the most important country houses built at that time in Scotland. Nowadays it is a List 'D' school. The parish church has a splendid Adam ceiling. The oldest church in north Fife is Moonzie—it is of uncertain age, but was extensively restored in 1882. It is sometimes called the 'visible' church, because it stands on top of a hill and may be seen from the road from Newburgh to Cupar. Beneath Colluthie Hill, Lords Cairnie Farm now stands on the site of a drained loch, reclaimed at the beginning of the nineteenth century. Lords Cairnie, or Earl Beardie's Castle, built about the middle of the fifteenth century by Alexander, fourth Earl of Crawford—he was known as the 'Tiger Earl' or Earl Beardie, because of the fierceness of his nature—is now a ruin. The keep or donjon was once surrounded with a defensive wall protecting the courtyard. According to the records of the Kirk Session, when the minister was ejected from his church in the late seventeenth century, the Great Hall of Earl Beardie's castle was fitted up as a meeting-place for him and his adherents until 1693, when they were able to move back into their own kirk.

Further north, on the coast road from Newburgh to Newport, is the little village of Flisk. The church of Flisk, a plain building in the simple eighteenth-century Scots vernacular, was put up in 1790. Built into a wall near the church is a Celtic serpent stone, no doubt related to the Celtic village that once grouped itself on Dunmhor. It is generally thought that this was a considerable settlement. The hill is now known as Norman's Law, a corruption of Northmen's Law, the Viking invaders having used it as a burial ground when their ships rode at anchor in the estuary of the Tay. Near here, too, is the impressive ruin of Ballinbreich, once the stronghold of the Earls of Rothes.

Beneath its overhanging walls lies one of the most beautiful stretches of the Tay. These reaches of the river were owned in the eighteenth century by Warren, son of Hugh of Abernethy, who gave four acres of Ballinbreich and the fishing rights on the estuary to the priory of St Andrews, his son later adding payment of ten shillings a year for Masses to be said for his parents. The parson of Flisk witnessed this charter.

Rathillet also has curious religious associations. The estate was given by Malcolm IV, in the twelfth century, to the Earls of Fife, who granted an annual rent of five pounds towards the support of the monastery of the preaching friars near Cupar, a sum paid up until the Reformation. In 1670 David Hackston heired Rathillet. On 3 May 1679, nine Covenanters, led by Hackston of Rathillet and Balfour of Kinloch, waylaid James Sharp, Archbishop of St Andrews, on Magus Muir, three miles west of St Andrews. Sharp was travelling in his coach with his daughter when the Covenan-

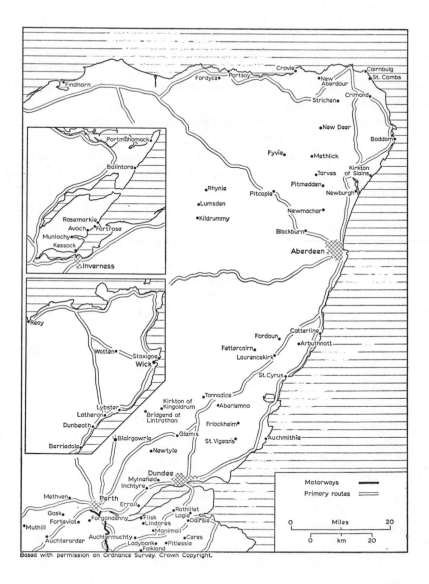

Based with permission on Ordnance Survey. Crown Copyright.

ters fired a shot through the coach window. Balfour of Kinloch rode up to confront the archbishop, telling him that they intended to take his life in God's name. "Save my life," said Sharp, "and I will save yours." "It is neither in your power to save us nor kill us," Balfour answered, and fired his pistol at him. Another Covenanter stabbed the archbishop with a pike, and wrenched the door open. Sharp staggered to the ground and was twice struck down whilst praying. "This," said his daughter, "is murder." To which came the fanatical reply: "Not murder, but God's vengeance on him for murdering many poor souls in the Kirk." "He is dead at last," said the footman. But another of the gang thrust a sword through his body until the blood gushed out, then said: "Now I am sure he is dead." Watching all this on horseback in the background, his cloak about his face, was Hackston of Rathillet. A year later, Hackston informed his judges in Edinburgh that he thought it "no sin to despatch a bloody monster". He was then himself despatched, his head being displayed on Edinburgh's Netherbow, and portions of his body at St Andrews, Magusmuir, Cupar, Burntisland, Leith and Glasgow. The Hackston or Hakerston family retained Rathillet until 1772.

A few miles along the road towards Wormit is Kilmany. With its pantile roofed cottages and hilly street with its church standing on a knoll, it has preserved its rural appearance. The church, built in 1768, had as one of its early ministers Thomas Chalmers of Anstruther, who was later to lead the Disruption, and became known as the "father of the Free Church of Scotland". The fourth Lord Melville, who was one of the Scots to bring William of Orange to the throne, is buried in Kilmany churchyard, also the burial place of the Melvilles of Muirdochairnie. Kilmany village has its own wooded glen, known as Goales Den. The result initially of trap rock disruption and then of continuous running water from the long-since-drained upper part of Motrayvale, Goales Den was laid out as a garden in 1825. On the southern shore of the Tay stands Balmerino. Above the village are the remains of a once great Cistercian abbey beneath the high altar of which William the Lion's widowed queen was buried. The place was burned by the English in 1548 and sacked by Knox's rabble in 1559. The

Elphinstones, as the occupants of the baronetcy, became Lords Balmerino. The first two to hold the title were sentenced to death, though not actually executed, but the sixth and last was beheaded on Tower Hill on 18 August 1746 for his part in the Jacobite rising. His death was watched by Horace Walpole and recorded in a letter to Horace Mann.

Wormit, at the Fife end of the Tay rail bridge, was a mere hamlet until the first stone of the original bridge was laid in July 1871. Opened in 1877, Thomas Bouch's bridge met disaster eighteen months later when on Sunday, 28 December 1879, the central girders collapsed in a storm while a train was crossing. The present bridge was opened on 20 June 1887. Now in effect a commuting suburb of Dundee, Wormit has one bright distinction. Alexander Stuart Stewart, the man who built many of its houses, installed electric lighting for those of his clients who wanted it, and made the village the first to have a primitive form of street lighting. The power came from a windmill which stood on Wormit Hill, supplemented in calm weather by the efforts of a steam engine. The cost to the consumers was only ten shillings (or 50p) per quarter, and there was no restriction of the electricity consumed. With an improved engine, this system lasted until 1930.

Tayport has long since had the status of a town. Originally known as Ferry-Port-on-Craig, a ferry plied from here for generations before the arrival of the bridge. It was for many years the home of the poet, polymath and scholar Douglas Young (1913–73), who named his house, appropriately, Makarsbield. Some centuries earlier Archbishop Sharp had his home at Scotscraig, a nearby estate thought to have been named by Sir Michael Scott of Balwearie, father of Michael Scott, the wizard.

Between Leuchars and Newport stands the hamlet of Pickletillem. Although the name derives from Pittentulloch, a Scotification of the Gaelic for 'hollow under the small hill', a local story insists that a joiner thereabouts ran short of nails of a certain size and sent his apprentice to the smith to collect a supply. Not having the size required, the smith handed the apprentice a bundle telling him to return to his master and "tak a pickle til him".

Leuchars is a village of considerable antiquity and interest. On the knoll of Castle Knowe, in the middle of what was once a marsh and later a moat, there once stood the castle of the Celtic chief Ness, whose father was Malcolm Canmore's Steward of Fife. Ness's daughter married Robert de Quinci, who set out on the Third Crusade in 1192, and died in the Holy Land. His son, Sayer de Quinci, Earl of Winchester, also a Crusader, was one of the signatories of Magna Carta. It is thought to be he who built, or at least completed, the church of St Athernase, which even in the reduced form it has come down to us retains enough of its Norman character—the semi-circular apse with its two arcades, the chancel, and much of the decorative work at the eastern end—to be a rare treasure. Unfortunately, seventeenth-century builders added a heavy tower and belfry to the Norman edifice.

Apart from the ornamented arches, the vaulted roofs and the carving on the capitals, there are some interesting memorials inside. The builder of the nearby mansion of Earlshall, Sir William Bruce, who died in 1584 having lived through Flodden, is commemorated here, as is Dame Agnes Lyndsay, wife of Sir William's great-grandson. It was a Bruce of Earlshall who is alleged to have paid a soldier a guinea to cut off the Covenanting leader Richard Cameron's head and hands, which he then carried to Edinburgh in a sack. He thus appears in Redgauntlet Castle in Scott's "Wandering Willie's Tale", "with Cameron's blude on his hand!" Earlshall itself is a fine example of a seventeenth-century house admirably restored and added to by Sir Robert Lorimer in 1891, his first major commission in Scotland.

Alexander Henderson had his first charge at Leuchars in 1618, when it was a fever-ridden countryside. Twenty years later, in Glasgow Cathedral, he became the first Moderator of the Glasgow Assembly of the Church of Scotland.

Two miles south is Guardbridge, which still has Bishop Wardlaw's fourteenth-century bridge that gave it its name, although a modern bridge carries traffic over the Eden. The making of paper now dominates this village. Near Leuchars, too, is the Royal Air Force airport which played an important part in the Second World War. It now operates an air-sea rescue service, amongst many other functions.

Logie, in a hollow of the hills, was the property of Sir John Wemyss, an ancestor of the Earls of Wemyss in the reign of Robert III. He is believed to have built the fifteenth-century Cruivie Castle, two miles to the north and now a ruin. Scott wrote his ballad "Laird of Logie" based on an incident in the life of one of the castle's owners.

The lands of Logie were bought in 1750 by Walter Bowman. He amassed a considerable library, and when he died left instructions that it had to be made available for consultation, but not withdrawal. Those using the books had to wash their hands with water provided. No women were to be admitted. Perhaps in these days of Women's Lib, it is just as well that the library has long since been dispersed.

Logie, little more than a hamlet, served the estate of Denbrae, owned by Sir William Fettes, who became Lord Provost of Edinburgh and bequeathed his name to the Edinburgh school. Dairsie is a pretty village with a curious church, built in 1621 by Archbishop John Spottiswoode, but stripped and rebuilt twenty years later "after the decent English fashion". The nineteenth-century historian Hill Burton called it, rather severely, "a piece of cold mimicry like the work of a cabinet maker rather than of the architect". Time, however, has mellowed our judgement. On a height above the Ceres Burn are the ruins of Dairsie Castle, where the Scottish Parliament met in 1335, and where Spottiswoode wrote much of his *History of the Church and State of Scotland*.

Round the eastern side of Cupar a four-hundred-year-old bridge built by Archbishop Beaton crosses the Eden, and the road winds through Dura Den to Pitscottie. Kemback, on the way, once had a church linked by Bishop Kennedy—whose memory is celebrated annually by the students in the Kate Kennedy pageant at St Andrews University—to St Salvator's at St Andrews when the college was founded in 1458. The present church, however, was built in 1814, after which the original one soon tumbled in ruins. The carved figure of a knight in armour, uncovered in recent years, is thought to have belonged to the tomb of Robert de Ferny, who lived in the latter part of the fifteenth century. Pitscottie, a hamlet in a dell, on the site of the farmstead bearing the name of the place,

Moniaive, Dumfriesshire, pleasantly enclosed by the hills around the Cairn valley, has associations with the last Covenanter martyr, James Renwick, and with Annie Laurie, who once lived in nearby Maxwelton House

The Merchant's Tower, one of many sixteenth-century buildings in Culross, Fife, a village now a show place of early Scottish domestic architecture

Falkland, Fife, with its medieval royal palace, where James V died shortly after hearing of the birth of Mary, Queen of Scots and James VI heard himself called "God's silly vassal" by the Reverend Andrew Melville

Drymen, Stirlingshire, in Strathendrick, has a panoramic mountain view as fine as anything in Scotland, and this parish church, built in 1771

Blanefield, Stirlingshire, in the Blane valley, originally had a calico print works but is now a commuter village nestling beneath the Campsie Hills

Killearn, Stirlingshire, north-west of the Campsie Fells, had its eighteenth- and nineteenth-century cottages preserved in the 1930s by the Killearn Trust, set up by a Glasgow businessman G. J. Innes

Port of Menteith, Perthshire, the tiny hamlet on Scotland's only natural lake, the Lake of Menteith, on the fringe of the Trossachs

Muthill, Perthshire, in wooded setting in Strathearn, was rehabilitated by the Earl of Perth after being burned by retreating Highlanders in 1715

Auchterarder, Perthshire, once a
Crown possession with a royal
residence was destroyed in 1716 by
the Earl of Mar and rebuilt as a
handloom weaving village making
linen. It is now the longest village
in Scotland

The Pictish symbol stone, one of
many to survive in the north,
preserved in the quaint village of
Fowlis Wester, Perthshire

The village of Glamis, Angus, built to serve the castle made famous by Shakespeare's *Macbeth* and more recently as the childhood home of Queen Elizabeth, the Queen Mother

Auchmithie, Angus, thought to have flourished in the eleventh century, is the 'Musselcrag' of Scott's *The Antiquary* and is built on a rock bank rising more than 100 feet above the beach

Gourdon, Kincardineshire, a nineteenth-century village with a good harbour and the first port in Scotland to adopt the diesel-driven fishing boat in the heyday of the steam drifter

Catterline, Kincardineshire, a picturesque fishing village on a cliff-top ridge named after St Catherine, where the artist, the late Joan Eardley, lived, and the present home of James Morrison

New Deer, Aberdeenshire, the largest of four villages founded by James Ferguson of Pitfour at the end of the eighteenth and beginning of the nineteenth centuries

Sandhaven, Aberdeenshire, a fishing village on the Moray Firth

had at one time a "countrie hous covered with strae and reide" which was the home of Robert Lyndsay, author of *The Chronicles of Scotland from 1436 to 1565*. Lyndsay of Pitscottie, a distant kinsman of Sir David Lyndsay, had an apt eye for detail and a vivid prose style, that make his somewhat fanciful account still well worth reading. We are, for instance, indebted to him for the story of the staged apparition at St Michael's, Linlithgow, designed, perhaps by Sir David, unsuccessfully to warn James IV against proceeding to Flodden. We also have from Pitscottie a description of the death-bed scene when James V heard that his wife had borne a daughter, the future Mary, Queen of Scots, rather than a son.

Ceres, a village on the left bank of the Ceres Burn, was originally called Cyrus after St Cyr, its patron saint before the Reformation. It has a well-organized folk museum created and looked after by the Central and North Fife Preservation Society. Ceres lies in the middle of a fold of hills, and has managed to retain its village green and humped-backed, centuries-old bridge. A statue, built into a wall in the centre of the village, the work of a Ceres man John Howie, represents the Reverend Thomas Buchanan, the last Church Provost of Ceres, who took up office in 1578, and was a cousin of the more famous George. The representation of the Battle of Dunfermline below it was discovered in the grounds of nearby Kirklands, and put in its present position in 1939. Ceres is one of Fife's all too few rural conservation areas. Apart from the ruined Craighall, the once-splendid Renaissance mansion and home of Sir Thomas Hope, Charles I's King's Advocate, there are also nearby the ruins of The Struthers and of Scotstarvit. Struthers Castle, near the hamlet of Craigrothie, once one of the greatest houses in Fife, is now a rickle of stones. Its full name was Auchtervthyrstruthyr, and it was the home of the Lords Lindsay of the Byre. Sir David Lyndsay knew its hospitality, and set one of the scenes of his poem on the life of Squire Meldrum in the castle. Cromwellian soldiers occupied it for three months in 1653. The square tower of Scotstarvit, in a valley two miles from Cupar, had as its most famous incumbent Sir John Scot of Scotstarvit (1585–1670). Sir John planned a survey of all the counties and islands of Scotland, and brought in Timothy Pont, minister of Dunnet,

H

to draw his maps. The Pont maps with Scot's descriptions were printed in Amsterdam by John Blaeu in 1654. The work made the authors famous throughout the centres of learning on the Continent.

The work by which Scot of Scotstarvit is perhaps better known today, if only by repute, was published eighty-four years after his death. It is called *The Staggering State of Scots Statesmen*. Broadly speaking, it has for its theme the highly probable proposition that, between 1550 and 1650, almost every politician achieved his position by fraud and trickery.

A guest at Scotstarvit must often have been Scot's brother-in-law, the poet William Drummond of Hawthornden. A dispute between Drummond's sister, Lady Scot, and his future mother-in-law, Dame Cunningham of the Barns, over a right of way to a midden, gave rise to Drummond's poem "Polemo-Middinia", a macaronic exercise in mock heroics the humour of which was doubtless much to Sir John's broad rural taste.

Still further up the valley of the Eden lies Pitlessie, celebrated in Sir David Wilkie's picture *Pitlessie Fair*. Wilkie was born in 1785 at the manse of Cults, a mile or so from the village. The house in which he saw the light was destroyed by fire in 1926, though the kitchen is said to have been included in the present house. The doocot and the north lodge survive. The faces of Pitlessie folk also did duty for another of his social canvasses, *Village Politicians*. Wilkie succeeded Raeburn in 1823 as Limmer to the King in Scotland, and seven years later succeeded Lawrence as Painter in Ordinary. After Wilkie's death off Gibraltar, and burial at sea, in 1841, a tablet was erected to his memory in the church of Cults. It reminds us that he served three monarchs: George IV, William IV and Queen Victoria. The square-looking church, built in 1793, has a font captured in the Crimea and brought to Fife by a local ship's captain. Though it suffered neglect and was substantially rebuilt in 1871, Crawford Priory was a Gothic mansion-house begun in 1813 by Lady Mary Lindsay Crawford, who succeeded to the Crawford Lindsay estates on the death of the twenty-second Earl of Crawford. Living in seclusion, she gathered around her an extraordinary collection of birds and animals. There were interesting interiors by David Hamilton and Gillespie Graham, but in recent years the building succumbed to dry rot and is now unfortunately only a romantic ruin.

From "St Andrews by the Northern Sea", round the coast by Fife Ness and through the East Neuk ports of Anstruther, Pittenweem and St Monance, to Elie, Largo and the shores of the Forth estuary, there are really no coastal villages left. All these pleasant red-pantiled places are now towns of varying sizes. Inland, however, there are still several villages worth visiting in the passing. Unpretentious hamlets like Arncroach and Carnbee, between which stands fifteenth-century Kellie Castle, restored by the Lorimer family—hamlets which even the observant motorist is through almost without noticing—are plentiful.

There is one other village hereabouts not only worth mentioning, but specifically worth visiting. Kilconquhar stands on the northern shore of Kilconquhar Loch. The village consists of one curving street. Its pantiled harled cottages and neatly cultivated gardens lead to the church of 1820 on a raised hillock at the end of the village. Though picturesque, the ruins of what was probably a simpler but more striking former church survive in the churchyard. The tombs of the Bethunes, who held the title of Lindsays of the Byres, may be seen in the remains of the walls. Kilconquhar Castle, damaged by fire in 1978, has been converted into flats.

Strange as it may seem, the loch was once used for the drowning of witches. According to tradition, the witch of Pittenweem met her end here when:

> They tied her arms behind her back
> An' twisted them wi' a pin,
> An' they dragged her to Kilconquhar Loch,
> An' coupit the limmer in.

This is, indeed, Lindsay country. The nearby mansion of Balcarres is the seat of the Earl of Crawford, now the head of the Lindsay clan. The third Earl of Balcarres, Colin, who died in 1722, was a Jacobite, though a cousin by marriage to William of Orange. In 1705 the third Earl founded the village of Colinsburgh, from which the gates of Balcarres Park may be seen. The fifth Earl, who married late in life, was the father of Lady Anne Lindsay (1750–

1825), who composed the song "Auld Robin Grey" in 1772, naming the subject of the song after an old Balcarres herdsman. She played a not unimportant part as an early recorder of conditions in what is now South Africa, where her husband, Andrew Barnard, was in political service, and she was a friend and unofficial confidential adviser to the all-powerful Henry Dundas, whose hand in marriage she once had the temerity to refuse.

Pleasant, too, are the views of the Fife landscape from the little village of Largoward, from which coal was once extracted to provide Falkland Palace with warmth in the days of James VI.

Kinross, formerly one of the smaller Scottish counties, possesses the striking feature of the Lomond Hills for background, and, lying to the west of them, Loch Leven. The related villages of Kinnesswood and Scotlandwell, on the western slopes of the hills, are served by Portmoak Church. Both villages, apparently known to the Romans, look across towards Benarty Hill. Andrew of Wyntoun (*fl.* 1400), the medieval poet chronicler, and John Douglas (d. 1574), the first tulchan Archbishop of St Andrews, were born in the parish.

Michael Bruce (1746–67) was born in Kinnesswood. Bruce was studying to be a minister, but died of consumption. He left a small volume of poems, from which his "Ode to the Cuckoo", regarded at the time as his best production, was filched by his friend, the Reverend John Logan, and published in his own name. Bruce, however, versified some of the Scottish paraphrases, and through these anonymous strains countless thousands of Scots have sung his most inspiring words without being aware that they were doing so.

> No strife shall rage, nor hostile feuds
> disturb those peaceful years;
> To plough shares men shall bend their swords,
> to pruning-hooks their spears.

The Reverend Ebenezer Erskine (1680–1754) ministered in the parish church from 1703 till 1733, when he founded the Secession College at Gairney Bridge. Dr Alexander Buchan (1829–1907), the originator of Buchan's Cold Spells, was also a native of Kinnesswood.

Blairadam, more of a hamlet than a village, owes its fame to

Blairadam House, built by William Adam (d. 1748), father of the still more famous architects, Robert (1728–92) and James (1721–92). The owner of Blairadam, the judge William Adam (1731–1839) was a lifelong friend of Sir Walter Scott. Together with seven others, they formed the Blairadam Club in 1816. They met on a Friday, and spent the next day riding to some scene of historical interest. It was just such a ride that gave rise to Scott's novel, *The Abbot*. Sunday was spent at home, Monday morning on another antiquarian excursion, and Monday afternoon on the return to Edinburgh in time for their appearances in court on Tuesday, their host being Lord Chief Commissioner of the Jury Court in Scotland. Attendance at church was in the nearby village of Cleish, a peaceful little village below the Cleish Hills. The building itself, the 'Kirk of Cleish Bothan' that features in the introduction to *The Abbot*, was badly damaged by fire in 1832, the year of Scott's death, the present building being erected within the outer walls. The village school of Cleish, built in 1834, had a schoolmaster celebrated by Burns:

> Here lie Willie Michie's banes:
> Auld Satan, when ye tak him,
> Gie him the schulin o' your weans,
> For clever deils he'll mak them.

But Cleish's most famous literary celebrity was Squire Meldrum, born at the House of Cleish in 1493, and celebrated in Sir David Lyndsay of the Mount's racy poem. The remains of Meldrum's house lie rather nearer Paranwell, a village formerly on the Queensferry to Perth road, though now by-passed and reduced to a few cottages. A bridge by the side of the original road, built in 1838 by William Adam at Scott's suggestion, commemorates an attempted ambush by the Earl of Rothes and his associates in June 1564, when they proposed to capture Lord Darnley, then accompanying his future wife, Mary, Queen of Scots. Mary, on her way to attend the baptism of a child of Lord and Lady Vincent Callender, had, however, been forewarned by Lindsay of Dowhill, and defeated the intention of the Confederate Lords by arriving earlier than she had announced.

Since Milnathort has for long been a market town, having outgrown village status by the time the poet Walter Chalmers Smith (1824–1908) ministered there in the 1850s, let us round off this chapter with a visit to the west of the county, where Crook of Devon stands on the banks of the River Devon. Burns celebrated the river in a somewhat facile song beginning:

> How pleasant the banks of the clear winding Devon,
> With green spreading bushes and flowers blooming fair.

Just beyond the village, the river plunges into a series of ravines, rushing through the Devil's Mill and lurching over the Cauldron Lynn. It passes beneath Rumbling Bridge, so called because the noise of the water was thought in the eighteenth century to resemble the sound produced by "heavy laden waggons on a rough road between reverberating heights". Surprisingly, in 1662 this peaceful village was the scene of five trials for witchcraft. Twelve witches and one warlock were accused of forming a 'coven'. A woman in her eightieth year died during the trial. Eleven were condemned and burnt to death on a nearby knowe. One woman, Agnes Pittendreich, got off on the grounds that she was pregnant.

Aldie Castle, which stands on a hill near the banks of the Pow Burn, to the south of the Crook of Devon, dates from the sixteenth century and was the seat of the Mercers. Tulliebole, on the road to Kinross, was begun by an Edinburgh advocate, John Halliday, in 1608, though it was later acquired by the Moncrieffs, a family who provided the legal profession with many of its luminaries, including three Lords of Session and Sir James Moncrieff, Lord Justice Clerk, raised to the peerage with the title of Baron Moncrieff of Tulliebole in 1874.

6

The Heart of Scotland

WHAT is sometimes curiously but inaccurately referred to as the 'Forth and Clyde Valley' (usually by weather men establishing the spreading presence of fog, these two great rivers having their sources many miles apart) or, alternatively, as the 'Heart of Scotland', links east and west. Whatever you choose to call it, Central Scotland takes in Dunbartonshire, Stirlingshire and Clackmannanshire. It also includes a few villages in Perthshire, since Perthshire, like Dunbartonshire, is partly a Highland county.

The first village to be passed by on the road from Glasgow to Dumbarton is Bowling, the western terminal of James Watt's Forth and Clyde Canal, now closed to through-traffic. It was constructed between 1768 and 1773, with John Smieton as the chief engineer. Milton is of interest because the first power-loom in Scotland was installed in its long-since-vanished cotton mill. To-day, most of it is new and climbs the slopes of the Kilpatrick foothills. As it happens, this book is being written in a house on Milton Hill, overlooking the Clyde.

Cardross, on the road to Helensburgh, the name of which derives from the Gaelic car-rois, 'curved point', once had a castle that stood on the north-western outskirts of Dumbarton. Here King Robert Bruce spent the last two years of his life, and here he died on 17 June 1329. The village church, built in 1826, was destroyed in a German air raid during the Second World War, though the tower has been preserved as a war memorial. The village itself is now an ever-growing commuting community.

Balloch, from the Gaelic *beul loch*,'the mouth of the loch', is a name that, like Milton and Kirkton, appears all over Scotland. The Dunbartonshire Balloch sits across the Lowland end of Loch Lomond where the Leven begins its short journey to the Clyde. With Balloch Castle and Park now in public ownership, it attracts many Glaswegians. From Balloch pier paddle-steamers plied throughout the nineteenth century and almost half-way through the twentieth, to provide a life-line to the Highland villages clustered about the loch shore, though in latter years only for pleasure-cruising. Behind Balloch, the land to the south is flat. Looking northwards up Loch Lomond, the hills of the Highlands shoulder either side of this splendid stretch of water that seemed to Tobias Smollett, himself born in Bonhill, to be preferred to "The Lago di Garda, Albano, De Vico, Bolsena and Geneva . . . a piece of water romantic beyond imagination".

Moving eastwards towards Stirling we pass the tiny village of Gartocharn. To have had the privilege of living in Gartocharn for more than a decade, as I did, and so easily to have been able to look upon Loch Lomond in its countless varying moods, is a matter for lifelong thanksgiving!

A few miles along the banks of the River Endrick, the road runs into Stirlingshire, with its many delightful villages, half Highland, half Lowland, set into mountainy prospects so delightful as to lift up even the dourest heart. Unlike more rugged prospects, the surroundings are human. The first of these villages is Drymen deriving, not from thirsty males but possibly from the Gaelic *drurm ridge*, though equally possibly simply a corruption of *drum*, after Drummond, the family who once owned the area. A conservation area, it centres upon an irregular village square. Most of its hostelries are old, though modernized; notably the Clachan Inn, which is eighteenth century, and the Buchanan Arms Hotel. The white church decorated with a contrasting colour, dates from 1771. Its predecessor was used as one of the points from which Rob Roy regularly collected the bribe-money he exacted for his protection services. Some gravestones from this time remain, the oldest dating from 1618. Buchanan, on the road to Balmaha, is a tiny though charming hamlet. Once the home of the Montroses,

Buchanan Castle, now a roofless shell, was put up by William Burn in 1854.

In the far distant past Drummonds and Montroses swopped their lands. Although the Montrose family still own Auchmar House and its lands, their connection, reaching back several centuries, has become more tenuous. The parish church, built in 1764, stands on a tree-sheltered knoll, and round it are buried the more recent Dukes of Montrose. The original parish kirk was on the island of Inchcailleach, on Loch Lomond, the ruins of which still survive. One stone is believed to mark the resting-place of St Kentigerna, an Irish missionary saint, who founded a nunnery there and died in 733.

Balmaha, on Loch Lomond, stands at the very gateway to the Highlands, by the entrance to the Pass of Balmaha, a gap in an outspill of Conic Hill, easily closed by Rob Roy and the Mac-Gregors in the warring days. The old manse was at one time the home of the much loved Lord Bannerman of Kildonan. In summer, yachts and motor boats speckle the shallow bay. A motor launch makes regular mail-trips round the islands in Loch Lomond.

In the valley of the Blane Water there are several villages popular with Glasgow commuters. Sheltered by the Campsies to the north are Blanefield and, the older of the two, Strathblane astride the junction of the A81 and A891. Its church, which dates from 1802, stands on the site of a previous building. Beneath the floor are said to be the tombs of Princess Mary, James I's sister, and her husband, Sir William Edmonstone of Duntreath. The Edmonstones are still in possession of Duntreath Castle.

Blanefield village, near the hill of Dumgoyne that marks the western end of the Campsie Fells, grew up to support a calico works long since vanished. It has become a dormitory village for those working in Glasgow. Killearn and Balfron, both conservation areas, lie on the western slopes of the Fintry Hills and Campsie Fells, with Fintry sitting between the two ranges. Killearn is near the junction of the Blane and Endrick Waters, the older part of it set on a ridge to the north of the more residential modern area. The present church, built by David Bryce and adorned with a tall spire, was intended as a memorial to a daughter of the Orr-Ewings of

Ballikinrain. An earlier church built in 1826 is now used as a community hall. The oldest of the three churches, now roofless, is surrounded by the graves of many local lairds and their families. There is a spectacular memorial obelisk to George Buchanan (1506–82), born at nearby Moss. Buchanan, who celebrated the wedding of Mary, Queen of Scots, with a Latin epithalamium, and was a cordially disliked tutor of James VI, had many of the narrower qualities of Scottish intolerance. He was to live to help incriminate the queen he had once celebrated with so-called 'evidence' that was no evidence at all at her English 'trial'. Round the square, dominated by the Black Bull Hotel, are pleasant eighteenth- and nineteenth-century cottages restored by the Killearn Trust, this being a village that set out to protect its own environment long before the official establishment of the concept of the conservation area. Killearn House, about a mile and a half to the south-west, was built in 1806 for the Blackburn family. They were succeeded by the Grahams of Killearn, one of whom in 1712, when factor to the Duke of Montrose, persecuted Rob Roy's wife, an affront that did not go unpunished. A quarter of a mile along the road to Balfron, at the hamlet of Blairessan, the Romans and Caledonians are said by tradition to have fought a great battle. Gartness, on the Endrick, once had a castle and still has the mill built from the castle stones. One of these stones in the wall of the mill is dated 1574. The Pot of Gartness is a waterfall in a dank cauldron created by a series of rocky ledges over which the river pounds and plunges. The mill, now ruined, was a home of John Napier of Merchiston (1550–1617), the inventor of logarithms. Balfron is much less old. It was founded by Robert Dunmore of Ballindalloch, who set up a cotton mill there in 1789. The village climbs steeply up a hill to the old hamlet called the Clachan, which has grouped itself round the church, at the highest point. The name derives from *baille-bhroin*, 'the town of mourning', legend clinging to the story that in distant times all its many children were killed by a raid of wolves. Still more improbable is the legend that claims the murderers of Archbishop Sharp first rested here as they fled from Magus Muir in a vain effort to escape.

The old village of Balfron is a conservation area. Real efforts have been made to replace some of its only moderately distinguished original housing with developments in a style of stone-faced pastiche. Unfortunately, it still has many between-the-wars urban-looking council houses of poor design.

Fintry—one of four villages with this name in Scotland—a village surrounded by hills though not a Highland one, has a modern hotel on the site of its ancient inn at the Clachan, the oldest part of the village. Although its parish church dates only from 1823, there was a church dedicated to St Modan on the site at the beginning of the thirteenth century. To the east of the village once lived the popular war-time Secretary of State for Scotland, Tom Johnston, who later played an important part in the early development of the successful North of Scotland Hydro-Electric Board. Newton of Fintry was set up in 1794 by Peter Spiers of Culcreuch as a model village for workers in his cotton mill. The mill failed and only the mill-lade survives.

Buchlyvie is another hilly village rising up from the southern edge of Flanders Moss. It has a spectacular long-range view across the Highland Line. Its North Church, one of three in the village, was built in 1751 by the Seceders. Part of the village dates from the late eighteenth century. The Red Lion Inn possibly has a seventeenth-century core. Like Balfron, Buchlyvie is basically a linear village on a rising hill.

Gartmore stands upon the foothills of the Ben Lomond range, and climbs a south to north slope. It faces south towards the Campsie Fells and east across the one-time swamp of Flanders Moss, through which the Romans built the first road. The village is a conservation area, but like so many potentially attractive villages, has had to fight off pressures from excessive modern developments that would have swamped the original size of the village. The church was built in 1790, but remodelled in 1872. The great house associated with the village was Gartmore House, for many centuries the home of the Cunninghame Graham family, of which the most famous was R. B. Cunninghame Graham, alias Don Roberto, writer, traveller, and one of the founder members of the Scottish National Party. He, however, made his home at Ardoch, on the Clyde, and Gartmore House became the home of the Cayzers, shipbuilding baronets. It is now an institution, like so many of its kind. Lower down the hill are the remains of the sixteenth-century castle of Gartmore.

Gartmore had churchly associations with the Port of Menteith, a hotel and tiny hamlet on the shores of the Lake of Menteith. This beautiful stretch of water mirrors Inchmahome Priory on an island at its heart. To the Augustinian priory, now a ruin, the infant Mary, Queen of Scots was brought when Henry VIII was invading Scotland in an attempt to force her marriage to his son. Amongst those buried here are R. B. Cunninghame Graham of Gartmore and Ardoch, and his South American wife, who died from an excess of cigarette-smoking.

Aberfoyle, standing at the foot of the Dukes Road which winds its way over the Menteith Hills to Loch Vennachar and the Trossachs, is a village that suffers from an excess of day-trippers. It is prettily situated on the upper Forth. A mile to the west of the present village, at the Clachan of Aberfoyle, was Jean McAlpine's Inn, where Rob Roy and his followers made merry. The modern Bailie Nicol Jarvie Hotel, at the centre of the village, has the famous Red Hot Poker, with which the worthy Bailie defended himself in Scott's *Rob Roy*. It hangs from a tree opposite the front door. Along the southward road over the humped-backed bridge across the Forth, is Kirkton, the scene in 1671 of a notable Highland feud over a christening. Nearby is the Covenanters Inn, named not after the religious Covenanters, but after those twentieth-century nationalists who in 1949 drew up here the Scottish Covenant on self-government that attracted more than two million signatures, and was a notable landmark in the modern advance towards the recovery by the Scots of their national identity.

Further east, and still skirting the Highland Line, Kippen, on the south of Flanders Moss, climbs a hillside by-passed by the Dumbarton–Stirling road. It has some good eighteenth-century cottages, Taylor's Building among them. Here occurred in 1691 the 'Her'-ship of Kippen', when Rob Roy and his men, having captured two hundred head of cattle on their way to a tryst at Buchlyvie, then attacked Kippen in passing and added all its livestock to their booty. Just as they were fording the Forth, a detachment of dragoons from Cardross came upon them. In the battle that followed the troops were routed. The vernacular gable and belfry of the original parish church survive. Built in 1691, the year of the Rob Roy affair, the bell, dated 1618, presumably comes from a still older building. The present church was built in 1825 and reconstructed in the present century. The landscape artist Sir D. Y. Cameron, who made his home in Kippen, associated himself with this restoration.

Gargunnock, on the slopes of the Fintry Hills, also climbs a steep street, and like Kippen, has a number of late eighteenth-century houses. The church, on higher ground to the east of the village, was built in 1774 and is an impressive building. Gargunnock House has a classical southern front, but is basically a tower house of the sixteenth century with a seventeenth-century wing. Once owned by the Seytons of Touch, it has for the past hundred years been the property of the Stirling family. No trace remains of Gargunnock Peel, which the poet Blind Harry caused Sir William Wallace to attack and capture from the English. Thornhill, on the northern side of Flanders Moss, is a large village the character of which has been mostly eroded by modern extensions. It adheres to its original street plan, and is of interest in that it was originally intended to be a village for resettled Highlanders after the 'Forty-five, the intention being that they could usefully drain Flanders Moss for employment. Doune, with its sturdy castle, still partly roofed, where the future playwright John Home was a prisoner during the 1745 rising, has grown into a small town. Pistol-making was a local industry for two centuries, introduced in 1645. Deanston, nearby, beside the Forth, was a planned industrial village originally based on its early nineteenth-century spinning mills, now converted to a distillery. It is a conservation area. We therefore pass through Stirling, climb the road that winds round the Wallace Monument, and take a look at the former County of Clackmannan, through which the Rivers Devon and Black Devon flow.

Logie and Blairlogie, lying at the foot of the Ochils with the peak of Dumyat behind them, are pleasant places. Logie has two churches, one dating from 1684, picturesquely ruined. In the parish church here the poet Alexander Hume (1560–1609) ministered, author of "Of the Day Estivall". Blairlogie Castle, now The Blair, dates from 1513 and was a seat of the Spittal family. Blairlogie, once regarded as a health resort, is made up of a delightful huddle of whitewashed houses set about leafy winding lanes.

Menstrie is now rather an ugly village, its few surviving red-pantiled cottages not numerous enough to balance poor twentieth-century development. Menstrie Castle, restored by The National Trust for Scotland, was the birthplace in 1567 of the poet and statesman Sir William Alexander, who became the first Earl of Stirling and a founder of Nova Scotia.

Tullibody and Cambus lie in the Devon valley. Tullibody has the remains of its traditional village south of the Stirling road. The village is somewhat scattered, though with a well-landscaped new housing scheme. The eighteenth-century mansion, once the home of the local laird, is separated by almost a mile from the parish kirk. The old kirk, built by David I in 1149, is a ruin. The stone flags of its roof were removed in 1559 by Mary of Guise's French troops, in a hurry to remake a bridge across the Devon that had been demolished by the Lords of the Congregation. Although it was afterwards re-roofed, its walls are now once again open to the skies. The Abercrombies of Tullibody House lie buried here, their most famous member being Sir Ralph Abercrombie, the hero of Aboukir. Cambus, with which Tullibody is usually related, is a quiet backwater where the Devon meets the Forth. It was once a busy place with a harbour and a mill, both worked by those who lived in its eighteenth-century cottages. Its nineteenth-century distillery has some buildings which dwarf the scale of the original village. Behind them, however, is Scotland's oldest surviving iron bridge, restored during European Architectural Heritage Year in 1975.

Stirling and Perth claim to be gateways to the Highlands. This is no mere meaningless outburst of touristic rivalry, because both claims are true. Stirling does, indeed, look towards the west, while Perth stands at the foot of the Perthshire Highlands to the north. In between these two towns are several villages more or less Lowland. Ashfield is another planned industrial community in the middle of the countryside, dating from the mid-nineteenth century, and developing in connection with a silk-dyeing mill. Braco, on the A822 Crieff road, was put up only in the second decade of the nineteenth century, although the parish church dates from 1780. It is a village clustered around the joining of two roads, at its most attractive in the vicinity of the clock tower of the ruined 1845 Free Church. Cattle fairs were once held in its rather uninteresting main street. Its great house, Braco Castle, two miles north of the village, is a much added-to sixteenth-century tower once owned by the great Marquis of Montrose's uncle.

Muthill, in Strathearn, further up the Crieff road, is almost a town, a well-preserved example of the old Scots burgh. There were Roman stations hereabouts at one time. Other warriors who took an interest in the place included the followers of the Jacobite Earl of Mar, who set it on fire retreating from Sheriffmuir in 1715. The name, which derives from moot-hill, hill of meeting, reminds us of its antiquity, an antiquity celebrated by the redstone tower of the ruined Celtic church which dominates the village. In the care of the Scottish Development Department, seventy feet high and saddle-roofed, it was a Culdee place of worship dating from the twelfth century. The ruined pre-Reformation church was built in 1430. Ada, wife of Sir Maurice Drummond, who died in 1352, an antecedent of the Drummond family, has her effigy in the chancel. Drummond Castle, two miles to the north-west, is the Scottish seat of the Drummond Willoughbys, Earls of Ancaster, the descendants of these early Drummonds. It is still a private house, though with a museum and an armoury. The chief charm of Muthill is its sense of unity, its winding main street lined by honest vernacular houses made out of locally quarried stone.

Moving across the A9, Greenloaning is rather a scatter of a village. But Blackford has an attractiveness the driver on the A9, lodged in a traffic jam at the height of the tourist season trying to get through its main street, is apt not to notice. Originally a ford on the nearby River Allan, its late eighteenth- and early nineteenth-century houses still give it a close communal feeling, particularly in the street to the south unaffacted by the heavy through-traffic. After Sheriffmuir, Mar's men burned much of the older village. It was once watched over by the 1617 church, standing on a knoll above the level crossing, but now ruined. The ruin of Ogilvie Castle, a mile to the south-west, was another Graham stronghold.

Auchterarder, from the Gaelic *uachdar-ard-thir*, 'upper high land', is an ancient burgh in Strathearn. It considers itself a town, but is really a long linear village, the longest, in fact, in Scotland. When some obnoxious Englishman was unfavourably comparing Scottish cities with English, Jamie the Saxt replied that he knew a Scottish town with fifty drawbridges, "a country village between Stirling and Perth called Auchterardoch", where there was "a large strand running through the middle of the town, and almost at every door there is a long stack or stone laid over this strand, whereupon they pass to their opposite neighbours; and when a flood comes, they lift their wooden bridges in case they should be taken away, and these they call drawbridges". Drainage in the place is now somewhat less rudimentary.

'Bobbing John', the Earl of Mar defeated at the skirmish of Sheriffmuir in 1715, also burned all of Auchterarder except one house. Its sloping street thus grew up again during the eighteenth and early nineteenth centuries. The literary-minded Edinburgh judge, Lord Kames, founded the Girnel (or Grain House), now a hall and library, next to the Town Hall, in 1790. An unusual war memorial provides a gate to the entrance of the old post-Reformation seventeenth-century church, only the seemly square tower of which still survives. Auchterarder Castle, a favourite hunting seat of Malcolm Canmore, that unifying monarch who brought much of what is modern Scotland together, stood a little to the north-west of the parish church, near the Gallowhill. Only a rickle of stones remain. The pre-Reformation church, a mile to the south-east, on the Kinkell road, dates from 1200 and was a shrine to St Mockessock. It is fast crumbling away, under the burdens of age and total neglect.

A row over the right of aristocratic or land-owning patronage in the Church broke out in Auchterarder in 1834, when a certain Mr Young was presented to the parish by the superior. This proved to be the first squaring up of religious opposites which eventually led to the Disruption.

Crovie, Banffshire, a remarkable early eighteenth-century fishing village in a rocky ravine traversed by a burn, one gable end of its houses facing the sea, the other a bank of the ravine

Pennan, Aberdeenshire, is inhabited by fishermen's families many of whose menfolk fish the distant waters of Norway and Iceland

The busy fishing harbour of Macduff, Banffshire, one of the safest havens in the Moray Firth

Portsoy, Banffshire, was a major commercial port in the eighteenth century, though its 1825 harbour now only knows pleasure craft and lobster-fishing boats. The village has been well restored, and is still famous for Portsoy marble

The seatown of Cullen, Banffshire, with its gaily painted cottage gable ends to the shore and a two mile stretch of sands that are said sometimes to sing

Findochty, Banffshire, an immaculately painted town, its harbour between two headlands

Fordyce, Banffshire, a village that has gathered itself round its castle built in 1592 and possessing an Academy with a boarding-house founded on a bequest from an Indian magnate

Findhorn, Moray, was once the chief port of Moray but is now a holiday resort, though since 1975 housing the Findhorn Foundation, which grows its own vegetables and specializes in crafts

Avoch, Ross and Cromarty, now a small fishing community on the south shore of the Black Isle

Fortrose, Ross and Cromarty, originally named Chanonry, has a ruined cathedral founded by David I

Rosemarkie, Ross and Cromarty, stands on the south shore of the Black Isle opposite Fort George and is now a holiday resort

Berriedale, Caithness, situated on the northern bank of the joining of the
Berriedale and Langwell Waters

Dunbeath, Caithness, dominated by the mass of Dunbeath Castle, a scattered village of considerable charm

Lybster, Caithness, one of the largest villages in the north-east was designed by Sir John Sinclair, author of the *First Stastical Account*, still having its legacy of spacious streets and dignified houses

Methven, another large village six miles north-west of Perth on the A85 from Crieff, overlooks the valley of the Pow Water. It wears a somewhat drab Scots look. This was Moubray land, until Sir Roger Moubray of Methven joined with the English in attacking Bruce at the Battle of Methven in June 1306. When Bruce had avenged his defeat and regained power, he gave the lands to the husband of his daughter, Marjory, Walter the High Steward.

Methven Castle as it now stands is a mid-seventeenth-century fortalice on a ridge to the east of the village. James IV gave it to his Queen, Margaret Tudor, who, after Flodden, married as her third husband Henry Stewart, and who procured from her son, James V, the title Lord Methven for her husband. She died here in 1540.

The church at the south end of the village stands on the site of a collegiate founding of 1433. The aisle that became the burying-place of the Smythe-Methvens is believed to have been built for Margaret Tudor, since one of its stones bears a sculptured Scottish lion. The church has an ugly tomb to Sir Thomas Graham, Lord Lyndoch, described as 'the hero of Barossa', who was born at nearby Balgowan House.

Gask, just over two miles north-east of Dunning, was the birthplace of the poetess Caroline Oliphant, Lady Nairne (1766–1845), the Oliphants having acquired their lands from Robert the Bruce. After the songs of Burns, more of Lady Nairne's songs survive in popular use than those of any other Scots song-writer. Prince Charles Edward Stuart spent the night of 11 September 1745 at the old house of Gask—celebrated by Lady Nairne's song "The Auld Hoose"—and left a lock of his hair behind, which became a family heirloom. The Hanoverians seriously damaged the house. It is now restored, somewhat over-ornately. The 'new' house was built in 1801. Like Gask, Findo Gask is not a village, though it has a pleasant eighteenth-century church.

South of the Earn lies Forgandenny, an attractive village three miles west of Bridge of Earn, which seems to have spread out so that the communal relationship of its houses has disappeared. Forgandenny Parish Church, much of it pre-Reformation in structure, has an eighteenth-century wing, now used as an organ-loft in memory of the Lords Ruthven of Freeland. Andrew Brooke, a

I

local Covenanting martyr, is commemorated by a stone in the porch.

Near the hamlet of Drum is Balmanno Castle, the Murrays' late sixteenth-century stronghold restored by the architect Sir Robert Lorimer.

Forteviot was once the capital of the Pictish kingdom of Fortrenn. Its ancient church, long since replaced, was allegedly built by Angus mac Fergus, King of Picts (731–61) and dedicated to St Andrew. Fergus, in the company of Achaius, King of Scots, was reputed to have been fighting a battle with Athelstan in East Lothian when they saw a white cloud in the blue sky shaped like a St Andrew's Cross. They vowed to make St Andrew patron saint of their country if victory was granted them. It was, and he is. Pictish ornaments from Forteviot are now in the Museum of Antiquities in Edinburgh, although the present church of 1778 retains a Celtic saint's bell and one or two Celtic stone relics. The village itself is now mostly nineteenth century; at the centre is a small group of English-style cottages and a village hall.

Perthshire lies partly in the Highlands and partly in the Lowlands, and it is not easy to draw a distinguishing line. But such places as Fortingall, at the mouth of Glen Lyon, the alleged birthplace of Pontius Pilate, Kenmore, where the River Tay emerges from its loch, Balquhidder, where Rob Roy is buried, and Callander, at the gateway to the Trossachs, clearly lie outside a Lowland survey. They are, of course, well worth a visit from the traveller who may find himself in their several airts.

Eastwards towards Angus, along the southern bank of the Tay, lies St Madoes, in the Carse of Gowrie. It has an attractive 1799 church. A little to the east is Robert Adam's Pitfour Castle, now converted into flats. According to one theory, the lands of Erroll were given by King William the Lyon to his butler, William de Haya, whose descendants, the Hays, became High Constables of Scotland in 1315 and achieved their Earldom in 1452. Another theory credits the Hays with a much more ancient lineage. In any case, Erroll is a substantial village, set out on a ridge and with an unusual triangular market-place. Gillespie Graham was responsible for the Gothic parish church built in 1831. At the top of the village is Erroll Park, its mansion rebuilt after the fire of 1874 that left its fifteenth-century predecessor a shell.

Inchtyre, further down the Carse, must presumably once have been islanded by the Tay, but now stands high and dry. It is a planned 'estate' village with a Gothic church dating from 1834.

Longforgan, a straggling village more than a mile long, was a dependency of Castle Huntly, which is now a Borstal but was built in 1452 by the then Lord Gray, and much added to later. It was sold to the eleventh Lord Glamis, who became the first Earl of Strathmore. A plaque on a cottage in the village commemorates the place where the young Wallace is said to have rested, fleeing from the slaying of the son of the English Governor of Dundee, Selby; the first blow in the Wars of Independence.

Mylnefield, a little inland, takes its name from the famous family, successive generations of whom became the King's Master Masons in the days before there was a profession of architects. It is now virtually a suburb of Dundee.

There remains the area north and north-east of Perth, between the Tay and the Grampian foothills. Stanley is an eighteenth-century planned village. It has a mill founded in 1785 on the advice of Sir Richard Arkwright. Towards Dunkeld, Spittalfield, a conservation area, is another planned community clustering round a village green. East towards Blairgowrie is Meikleour, with its grand Victorian mansion by David Bryce beside the Tay and the tallest beech hedge in Britain. The village is outstandingly picturesque. Just across the Tay, Kincloven prettily groups its 1848 church in Romanesque revival style, the manse and a few houses.

7

East and North-East

NORTH of the Tay, the Lowlands fringe to the east of those mountains that form the spine of Scotland. In Angus, the glens of Isla, Prosen, Clova, Ogilvy, Lethnot and Esk run down from the Grampians. This is the area around the Sidlaw Hills. Fertile Strathmore reaches northwards towards the sea. There are also a flatter coastal strip, and the central heartland of Angus.

Many travellers reach Angus from the west, coming to it along the north bank of the Tay. Invergowrie, on the Tay estuary, is now a rather unattractive village; indeed, almost a suburb of Dundee. It has a ruined church, fifteenth century in origin, but said to have succeeded an eighth-century church founded by St Curitan. The Invergowrie Stone, now in the National Museum of Antiquities, is a Pictish cross-slab, decorated on one side with clerics surveying a dragon in understandable astonishment, and more conventional Celtic patterning on the other. Previously it had been built into the pre-Reformation ruins. On the shore nearby are the Yowes of Gowrie, two boulders about which Thomas the Rhymer wrote:

> When the Yowes o' Gowrie come to land,
> The day o' judgment's near at hand.

Happily, judgment has remained securely far off for several centuries.

Clustered around Dundee, now circled by a by-pass road, are several villages almost absorbed by the city. Muirhead of Liff is such a place, though Benvie, a mile to the south-west, is still an agricultural place, with a Celtic cross-slab gravestone from the seventh century in the graveyard of the badly ruined church. The scattered village of Kirkton of Strathmartine also has a number of Pictish stones in the graveyard of an old church, as well as the tombstones of the Ogilvys of Inverquharity. The Strathmartine Stone, taken from the grounds of the Regency-type house where an earlier fortalice once stood, is now in Dundee Museum.

Kirkton of Auchterhouse, to the north-east, has a one-time mill and a parish church dating from 1775, but incorporating pieces of an edifice of 1630. An ancient stone font is still in use, and it is a pleasing kirk. Its 'big house', a late sixteenth- and early seventeenth-century baronial mansion, appears to have been built by Sir John Stewart, son of the Black Knight of Lorn who married the widowed Queen, Joan Beaufort; she who, in youth, inspired the captive James I's beautiful poem "The Kingis Quhair". After several changes of hands, the castle came to the Ogilvys, Earls of Airlie. Wallace is said to have sheltered in a ruined tower which bears his name.

The hamlet of Kellas, or Hole of Murroes, and Murroes itself, groups prettily round its parish church, castle and farm from which the village has now disappeared.

Monikie, eight miles or so north-east of Dundee, stands at the west end of two of Dundee's reservoirs. It has a large granary, which stores grain for local distilleries. Kirkton of Monikie has a dull-looking church built in 1812. Craigton, at the east end, is a pleasant though scattered little village. The curious tower, known as the 'Live and Let Monument', was put up by the tenants of the re-created first Lord Panmure in 1839, the fourth Earl having suffered forfeiture for his Jacobite activities. It is visible from the village, a landmark to mariners and a vantage point over seven counties. On the same hill is the Camus Cross, a Christian Celtic monument, the original purpose of which, legend claims, was to mark the grave of a Danish king killed in battle by Malcolm II in 1010. More prosaically, Newbigging was built to house workers in the Omachie quarries, from which came the once-famous Arbroath paving stones.

The cross-roads village of Muirsdrum carries the roads to Carnoustie and to Arbroath. This was once the country of the Maule-Ramsays, Earls of Dalhousie. Panmure, their great seventeenth-century house rebuilt by David Bryce in 1832, has gone completely. Almost on the shore, the mansion of Panbride stands on land once owned by the ancestors of the historian Hector Boece or Boetius. The Earls of Panmure are buried at the east end of the seventeenth-century parish church. The fishing hamlet of East Haven is becoming increasingly a dormitory suburb for Dundee, while West Haven has been incorporated into Carnoustie.

Barry, nine miles east of Dundee, on the Buddon Peninsula between Monifieth and Carnoustie, has an attractive older part, lying in the den of Pitlare Burn, with a former mill and a roofless church as well as a cluster of cottages. On the A94, Coupar Angus to Forfar road, is Meigle, a cross-roads village with a museum that specializes in Pictish stones.

There are no villages of outstanding interest between Dundee and Coupar Angus. But on the A927 from Muirhead to Alyth is Newtyle, a planned village on the slopes of the Sidlaws, offered for feu by Lord Wharncliffe of Belmont Castle, Meigle, in 1832, a development designed to coincide with the construction of the Dundee–Blairgowrie railway line. It has the oldest railway station in Scotland, dating from 1836, though now converted to a barn.

Alyth and Kirriemuir are both small towns, the interest of the former lying in the attractiveness of the burn running through its main street, the fame of the latter resulting from its having been the birthplace of Sir J. M. Barrie. Northwards lie the hills, the mountains reaching behind Alyth. In autumn wave after wave of heather can be seen stretching almost to Braemar.

Behind and between the two Angus towns lies Bridgend of Lintrathen and Kirkton of Kingoldrum, picturesquely situated between whinny hills. The former is a scattered hamlet with a plain-looking little church, put up in 1803 in a graveyard where a Pictish stone still survives, built-in near the door. Nearby is woody Loch Lintrathen, one of Dundee's main reservoirs. Around the village are spectacular waterfalls, particularly those to the west, on the River Isla, at Bridge of Craigisla.

It was through a territorial association with Lintrathen that the Ogilvys were first known, their peerage later associating them with neighbouring Airlie, or Errolly, as it was once called. It stands in a seemingly impregnable position above the meeting-place of the Isla and Melgam Water. However, in Covenanting times it fell to the Marquis of Argyll in 1640—an action inspiring the ballad "The Bonnie Hoose o' Airlie"—who personally led the demolition work. Balladry, it seems, lies behind the supposed turning-out from Airlie of Lady Airlie, an incident actually occurring at Forfar Castle, further up Glen Isla. Behind the ruins stands the house which succeeded the old castle.

Kirkton of Kingoldrum stands at a road junction by a bridge over the Cromrie Burn, and is a curious blend of ancient and modern. When the old church was being taken down to make way for the present 1840 structure, Pictish stones were found embed-ded in the structure. Part of one of these stones is now in the National Museum of Antiquities in Edinburgh, where is also housed the bell of a Celtic saint, found at Kingoldrum. Balfour Castle, to the south, though said to have been built by Cardinal David Beaton for his secretly wed wife—or "chief lewd" as Knox pleasantly called her—Margaret Ogilvy, is now thought to be older and to have been an Ogilvy possession for rather longer. By pro-clamation of Alexander III, as a former possession of Arbroath Abbey, the Forest of Kingoldrum could not be used for hunting or cutting wood, except with the abbot's permission.

One of Scotland's several Ruthvens—the name is pronounced 'Riven'—lies on the road between Alyth and Kirriemuir, where it crosses the Isla over a modern bridge. Alongside is an older, lower-level bridge that has done duty from the seventeenth century. In-side the 1857 church, uphill and upstream, two small Celtic crosses are built into the west gable. The church bell, cast in 1735, came from the wooden warship *Enterprise*. The ancient Crawford-owned castle, downstream, was removed, except for one tower, when the present eighteenth-century mansion was built by the Ogilvys of Coul.

Glamis owes its worldwide modern celebrity not so much to the handsome red sandstone keep of the Lyons, Earls of Strathmore, as to the fact that King George VI married Elizabeth Bowes-Lyon, a daughter of the house. The six-storeyed keep, decorated with angle-turrets, parapets and dormers, has three-storeyed flanking wings and towers, adding to its mellow impressiveness. Basically, it dates from the fifteenth century, though it incorporates several later and considerable additions. Its outstanding features include the great hall, with its huge fireplace, mural chambers and fresco paintings, the chapel with its murals restored in our own day, and the vaulted crypt or secret chamber, filled with the cold of savage legend.

The village, a conservation area, is a splendid example of a place that grew up specifically to serve its great house. Now happily by-passed by north-bound traffic on the A94, its tree-lined street and lanes bordered with old houses are freed at last from decades of traffic annoyance. Its well-restored church, which stands near the site of a former cell of Celtic St Fergus and a later medieval church, dates from 1793. The Glamis Stone, a ten foot high Pictish cross-slab and symbol stone, sometimes erroneously dubbed 'King Malcolm's Stone' in the belief that Malcolm II was slain here, is to be found in the manse garden south of the church. Other ancient stones survive in the vicinity, notably the Cossans Stone, isolated in an open field two miles to the north. It is in the care of the Scottish Development Department. The National Trust for Scotland's fascinating Angus Folk Museum in Kirkwood, a row of seventeenth-century cottages with roofs of stone slabs, contains a varied collection of farm and domestic bygones.

At the foot of Glen Ogil is Tannadice, a worn-looking little village on a slope north of the South Esk. Its 1846 church, which replaced a pre-Reformation chapel that was a rectory of St Andrew's Cathedral, has an old font in the vestibule.

On the B9134 road linking Forfar and Brechin lies Aberlemno— its name deriving probably from *abhir-leumnach*, 'confluence of the leaping stream'—worth a visit for several reasons. The farm hamlet of Crosston, on a loop to the north of the village, is the place to make for to see three of the four local Pictish stones. Two are cross-slabs, all with intricate Celtic decorative pattern-work and one with horsemen and dogs. The oldest has serpent and mirror-and-comb symbols. The fourth, and most impressive, is in the kirkyard of the parish church, a little to the south. It has interlaced beasts on one side, horsemen, hunters and warriors on the other.

The little church itself, reconstructed in 1722, has a gallery on three sides and some old family box-pews. Brightly painted, it reaches back to the days before that sentimentalizing of religion induced by Victorian material prosperity, with its double standards.

Nearby are Melgund and Flemington Castles, the former probably put up by David Beaton, Cardinal, Archbishop and Chancellor of Scotland for his Ogilvy wife, but now in the possession of the Elliots of Minto, the other a roofless seventeenth-century fortalice last used by an ejected eighteenth-century Episcopalian clergyman, the Reverend John Ochterlony, when already a ruin, to minister to his followers.

Moving back towards Arbroath and the coast, the curiously named village of Friockheim lies at the junction of the A932 and A933, a village with two long main streets. *Frioch*, or *fraoch*, means 'heather' in Gaelic. Now pronounced 'Frickham', the village stands on the banks of the Lunan Water, which flows to the sea in Lunan Bay, popular with holidaymakers.

Behind Arbroath is St Vigeans, designated an outstanding conservation area, once a village on its own but now almost engulfed by the neighbouring town. It is said to derive its name from that of the Columban St Fechan, Abbot of Fobhar in Ireland, who also gave his name to Ecclefechan in Dumfriesshire. The old village has a famous red sandstone church, in part dating from 1100 though altered in the thirteenth, fifteen and nineteenth centuries, the 1872 restoration adding a chancel and north aisle.

In the cottage museum below the mound on which stands the kirk, the Scottish Development Department has preserved an extensive collection of Pictish stones, thirty-two in all. The most famous is the ninth-century Drosten Stone, named after a king of the Picts. A typical cross-slab, it carries hunting scenes and vivid animal pictures on one side, an angel and some strange-looking animals biting each other's tails on the other. A close look at it provides an oddly disturbing experience out of Scotland's largely mysterious Pictish past.

Two miles west of Arbroath is the village of Aberelliot, corrupted now to Arbirlot, on the Elliot Water. It is another conservation area, a picturesque place once famed for smuggling, a trade it apparently lost due to carelessness in paying the providers for their illicit goods. Its parish church, though basically ancient, was re-built and enlarged in 1832. South, and seawards, is Kellie Castle, a sixteenth-century fortalice of the Ochterlonys, bought by the Maule-Ramsay family in 1679 for £11,000 scots. The family re-stored it from a near ruinous condition just over a century ago. A little to the north is the conservation area village of Auchmithie, further up the coast. It is an easy cliff-walk from Arbroath, by former smugglers' caves with names like Elephant's Foot, Needle's Eye, Dickmount's Den and Deil's Head. Auchmithie is said to have been in existence as long ago as the eleventh century. It is the 'Musselcrag' of Scott's novel, *The Antiquary*.

On the A92 between Arbroath and Montrose is the village of Inverkeilor, on the edge of the valley of the Lunan Water. It has a parish church of seventeenth-century origin, with eighteenth- and nineteenth-century additions, in the oldest part of which is the burial aisle of the Carnegies, Earls of Northesk.

Ethiehaven, hidden away at the foot of the great sea cliffs dom-inated by Red Head on the southern arm of Lunan Bay, is a former fishing village on a ridge above the sea.

Between Montrose and Inverbervie there was once a large village, Miltonhaven. It was washed away in 1792, during exceptionally high tides whipped up by an easterly gale. St Cyrus, which replaced it, a large village with a good bathing beach, grew out of the com-ing together of several hamlets, its growth further stimulated by the erection of the bridge over the Esk in 1775.

Seagreens, a little to the north, has declined from its former village status to a mere handful of cottages, but the brick-vaulted ice-house for the storage of fish, of a type once common in Scottish ports, still survives there.

From St Cyrus, we move up the coast to Kincardineshire, a dis-trict of large upland farms once wearisome working, but now, thanks to modern technology, far removed from the toilsome wrestle with the elements that features in Lewis Grassic Gibbon's powerful trilogy *The Scots Quhair*. Johnshaven is another village with a still attractive harbour and eighteenth-century fishermen's dwellings.

J. Leslie Mitchell (Gibbon's real name) is buried in Arbuthnott churchyard. Arbuthnott has given its name, probably derived from *abhirbothennothe* 'bothy at the Neithe's confluence' to a distinguished Scottish family whose members have included Sir Robert Arbuthnott, who in 1505 built the chapel of St Mary's, attached to St Ternans Church near the village (restored in 1890 after a serious fire) and the famous wit of Queen Anne's reign, Dr John Arbuthnot.

Between St Cyrus and the town of Stonehaven is the bustling little town of Inverbervie with its pretty village port of Gourdon. Both have long since outgrown village status, though the local fishing fleet has declined sadly since the days when more than a hundred boats put out to sea. Hercules Linton, the designer of the record-breaking sailing ship *Cutty Sark*, was born in Inverbervie in 1836.

Northwards, beyond the headland of Bervie Brow, stands Kineff, and near it, Dunnottar Castle. When Cromwell's commander, Major-General Morgan, was besieging this castle in which the Honours of Scotland had been hidden for safe keeping when the 'Protector' overran Scotland, hunger eventually forced the lieutenant-governor, George Ogilvy, to surrender. Just before he did so, Mrs Christian Grainger, the wife of the Reverend James Grainger of Kineff, obtained permission from General Morgan to visit Mrs Ogilvy, arguing that such a distinguished soldier would surely not make war on women. She and her servant were thus allowed access to the castle. On the way back, she smuggled out the Scottish crown under her skirts, and got her servant to bring out the sword and sceptre wrapped in lint to look like a distaff. Safely back at Kineff, the Honours were hidden in a box bed, and later buried by night underneath the pulpit of the church, where they remained until the Restoration. As is so often the case, the brave Graingers received a paltry sum in reward, but Ogilvy was given a baronetcy while the owner of Dunnottar, Sir John Keith, the Earl Marischal (who, being in enemy hands, had played no part in the issue) was made Earl of Kintore and given a pension. The one-time royal seat of Kineff Castle is now a much worn ruin. A hoard of English coins was unearthed here in 1837, presumably left by an enemy garrison. The historic church, rebuilt in 1738 and restored in 1876, is no longer needed to serve so tiny a hamlet and wears a deserted look, though still occasionally used and much visited. It would be a sorry disgrace to Scotland if it were ever allowed to fall into disrepair and ruin!

Dr John Arbuthnot, the friend of Pope and Swift and physician to Queen Anne, spent part of his youth at Kingshornie. The Arbuthnots once owned Fiddes Castle, two miles west of Barras, an L-shaped sixteenth-century fortalice. It was restored from a near-ruinous state in recent years. A mile to the north of Fiddes is the farm of Clochnahill, from where Burns's father, William Burnes, set out to farm in Ayrshire. Three miles from Kineff, scattered about the top of a cliff, is the fishing village of Catterline, anciently Katerin, its little harbour beneath and the solitary stack of Forley Craig offshore. The 'best creek in the parish', it was called in 1700, and 'a notorious smugglers' haunt'. As a result, a coastguard 'Watch House' was built in 1750. It was here that the painter Joan Eardley (1921–63) spent her last years and, by creating many masterpieces, gave the place a celebrity of the imagination, through her reconstruction of the local coastline and seascapes. In 1970, a Bronze Age stone cist was found, dating from 1500–2000 B.C. and containing the skeleton of a boy aged about five.

Crawton, another deserted inconvenient cliff-top fishing village with a stony beach, has hard by it a spectacular waterfall tumbling into the inlet of Trollachy.

Inland, six miles north of Brechin, on the B966, is the pleasant village of Edzell, at the north-east end of Strathmore and on the west bank of the North Esk. This village, with its broad street and rectangular pattern, wears the look of the nineteenth century. It is, indeed, a planned village, feued by Lord Panmure in 1839. Modern Edzell was once called Slateford, the previous Edzell village having been situated at the mouth of Glen Lethnot, by Edzell Castle, the former church and the old kirkyard. The re-location was made when the church with its distinctive belfry came to be rebuilt in 1818 on a new site.

The traveller who approaches Edzell from the south comes upon a memorial arch, not unlike the Queen Victoria Jubilee Arch at Fettercairn, five miles away. The Edzell arch, however, commemorates the fifteenth Earl of Dalhousie, who died in 1887 and whose family has owned much of the area since 1715. Apart from the ugly Inglis Memorial Hall in the main street, the village has few scars, the modern housing scheme off Church Street being a model of its kind. Edzell, still an agricultural centre, possesses its own common land.

The village takes its name from ruined Edzell Castle, a mile up the side road to Glen Lethnot, past Mains of Edzell, a farm with a fine early seventeenth-century dovecot. The ruins of the castle are almost as imposing as those of Dunnottar. The donjon keep is the oldest part, much of the rest, including the great hall, being added in the late sixteenth century. The walled garden enclosure, or pleasance, still has its attractive little early seventeenth-century summer-house, roofed and entire, in itself a miniature castle. It was put here by Sir David Lindsay, Lord Edzell of Session in 1604, and was based on designs copied from Nuremburg.

Edzell belonged to the Glenesks, and then to a branch of the Stirlings that came to an end with two daughters about the middle of the fourteenth century. One of them married Sir David Lindsay of Crawford in 1357, and became the mother of the first Earl of Crawford. According to tradition, the Lindsays lost Edzell because they hanged two dumb gypsy brothers for poaching. Their mother prophesied death by nightfall for Lady Crawford, and thereafter, for her husband, a death to make him "shrink with fear". Such being the power of gypsies in those days, Lady Crawford died that same evening, while a year later her husband was torn to pieces by wolves, believed by some to be the reincarnated spirits of the hanged brothers.

In 1562 Mary, Queen of Scots visited Edzell and held a Privy Council. Cromwell garrisoned it in 1651. In 1715 the Lordship of

Glenesk was sold to the Earls of Panmure, whose Jacobite activities led to a visit from the Argyll Highlanders in 1745 and the destruction of the castle. The Lindsay vault, in the ruined old parish church of St Laurence, survives intact.

Fettercairn, another large village which features in Andrew of Wyntoun's *Cronykil* as "Fettyrkerne" and in Holinshed as "Fethercane", 'the cairn on a green hillock', lies five miles up the B966. It is entered through the red stone arch commemorating Queen Victoria's arrival in the village in 1861. On this occasion she stayed incognito at the Ramsay Arms, where, as she herself relates in schoolgirlish prose, "there was a very nice drawing-room, and next to it the dining-room, both very clean and tidy, then to the left our bed-room, which was excessively small, but also very clean and neat. . . . We dined at eight, a very nice clean good dinner." In Fettercairn's wide central square stands the mercat cross from Kincardine, which ceased to exist as a village about 1600, when the seat of administration moved to Stonehaven. By then, Mary, Queen of Scots had already destroyed its castle on her northern expedition against the power of the Gordons. In 1670 a finial and sundial bearing the Earl of Middleton's coronet and initials, and carrying an ell measurement standard, was added to the original octagonal shaft. The parish church, though dating from 1804, stands upon a sixteenth-century vault. Fettercairn has a distillery at Nethermill, to the north-west, built in 1824. Fettercairn House, for five centuries a seat of the Middletons, was built in 1661. Its builder, the most famous of the family, was the Civil War General Middleton (1610–73), created Earl of Middleton at the Restoration. His son forfeited the estate in 1777, and it passed by purchase to Sir John Wishart Belsches. His daughter, Williamina, caused Sir Walter Scott to fall in love with her, but she deserted him in favour of the banker Sir William Forbes. The estate passed through the female line to Lord Clifton, the English peer who at present owns it.

Balbegno Castle, on the other side of the village, is another interesting sixteenth-century fortalice with a farmhouse attached to it. Given by James IV to Andrew Woods, the family who had been hereditary keepers of Kincardine Castle, five generations later it was sold to the Middletons.

A curious story about the last of the Woods is extant. It seems that he made a bargain with the second Earl of Middleton that whoever should die first would communicate to the survivor a report on the conditions to be found in the hereafter. Woods died in battle and in due course appeared in a vision to the Earl, then a prisoner in the Tower of London. Woods's report ran:

> Plumashes above, Gramashes below,
> It's no wonder to see how the world doth go!

Like most information from supernatural sources, these strange observations seem surprisingly trite.

Laurencekirk, in the Howe o' the Mearns lies along the A94. It was laid out in dull local red sandstone in 1765 by the Scots Law Lord, Francis Garden of Troup, Lord Gardenstone. The Episcopal church is also his creation, the parish church, on the site of the former Kirkton of Conveth not being built until 1804. The Masons' Lodge dates from 1779. A seventeenth-century tombstone of the Stiven family, founders of Laurencekirk's once-famous snuff-box industry, survives. Like its snuff-box manufacture, the village's linen-making industry has gone, although weaving has revived in a small way at the village of Luthermuir, to the south-west.

Thomas Ruddiman, who rose to be Keeper of the Advocates' Library and a famous grammarian and scholar, spent from 1695 to 1700 as schoolmaster at Laurencekirk, then the hamlet of Conveth. James Beattie, the poet of "The Minstrel" and an unsuccessful philosophical opponent of David Hume, was a native of nearby Barrowmuirhills.

Fordoun, four miles east of Laurencekirk, from where John Fordun, author of the fourteenth-century *Scotichronicon* came, though once a burgh, now consists only of a substantial farmhouse. The kirkton, called Auchenblae, a mile to the north, climbs a hill by the Luther Water. A large and attractive village, it once had a flax-spinning mill, now long disused, and its Paldy Fair—named after St Palladius whose chapel stood by the waterside at the foot of the hill—used to be an important festivity. The present Gothic edifice dates from 1829, though its ruined predecessor of 1244, once called the Mother-Church of the Mearns, lingers on in the kirkyard. St Ternan, a local aristocrat who took to religion, is thought to have brought Bishop Palladius's bones here from Ireland. Here, too, is a good Pictish slab, now set into the wall at the back of the later church. Monboddo, near Auchenblae, reduced and restored to its seventeenth-century size, was the birthplace in 1714 of James Burnett, who became an eccentric judge under the title of Lord Monboddo. He anticipated Darwin, believing that human beings were descended from apes. However, Monboddo also believed that children were born with tails, a conspiracy of midwives ensuring the removal at birth of the tell-tale evidence.

Drumlithie, seven miles south-west of Stonehaven, set back from the road, owes its attractiveness to its haphazard groupings, and its winding lanes. It has what looks like a Brechin-type round tower, although this one was, in fact, put up only in 1770 to house the bell regulating the working hours of its weavers.

The great glen of the Dee moves up through Banchory and Aboyne, towards the Deeside Highlands. As with the glens of Angus, the villages in these regions are plainly Highland, even although their connection with the Gaidhealtachd, and those who might be regarded as the indigenous Highland people, has long since receded. Indeed, the Lowland belt of the north-east, up which we are making our way, was in distant days Scotland's second frontier, where a Gaelic and a Norse-influenced Scots culture confronted each other as surely as did the English and Scots along the national border. One sign of this affinity of frontiers is the fact that the Northern ballad heritage, with its news-carrying tales of forays, attacks and burnings, is at least as rich, and—as it has come down to us—in some ways more authentic than the better-known treasury of border balladry, preserved and probably refined by Sir Walter Scott and his fellow-workers for *The Minstrelsy of the Scottish Borders*.

There is evidence aplenty of the influence the Howe o' the Mearns makes on those born within its ambience. Lewis Grassic Gibbon's *A Scots Quhair* has the inborn strength of its characters bent and embittered by the struggle with the land. The progressive weakness of the trilogy arises out of its author's increasing preoccupation with fancied crypto-Communistical Druidism. But the 'speak' of the countryside sings unforgettably through Gibbon's prose. In verse, too, Violet Jacob captures the nature of the haunting that this countryside, unsympathetic perhaps to eyes accustomed to a more relaxed scene, exercises over those who belong to it.

> London is fine, an' for ilk o' the lasses at hame
>> There'll be saxty here,
> But the springtime comes an' the hairst—an' its aye the same
>> Through the changefu' year.
> Oh, a lad thinks lang o' hame ere he thinks his fill
>> An' his breid he airns—
> An' they're thrashin noo at the white fairm up on the hill
>> In the Howe o' the Mearns.

As we move into Aberdeenshire, the villages become so numerous that it is impossible even merely to mention the majority of them in a work of this compass. Many of them, in fact, are unremarkable individually, although they add collectively to the unique quality of this farming landscape, now on its seaboard presented with yet another frontier, the late twentieth-century world of North Sea oil.

Proceeding up that part of this frontier running more or less along the valley of the Dee west of Ballater to the town of Huntly, Newkirk—or Kirkton of Logie-Coldstone to give it its other name—is little more than a scattered hamlet, though Tarland, to the east along the B9119, is a sizable village of character that still manages to support a thriving annual August agricultural show. Its parish church is a granite building dedicated to St Moluag in 1870, replacing the roofless kirk in the old graveyard, near the pleasant square. There is a monument in the square to the Scottish fiddle-music composer Peter Milne, and a well with Celtic decorative work, put up in 1913 to commemorate one Francis Donaldson, pleasing in itself even if it seems to have failed in its pious purpose.

Near Tarland are the headquarters of the well-known Mac-

K

Robert Douneside Farms. The House of Cromar, once the seat of that Marquis and Marchioness of Aberdeen who called their collective memoirs, *We Twa*, is now the R.A.F. Rest Centre, Alastrean House. This was endowed by Lady MacRobert after her three sons had been killed in World War II. At the nearby farm of Culsh, on the A974, is an underground Pictish souterrain weem, or storehouse, in which, uncharacteristically, it is actually possible to stand up. It is in the care of the Scottish Development Department. Migvie, an attractive hamlet three miles or so to the northwest, has a pretty little church dating from 1777, dedicated to St Finan.

Kildrummy, where the A97 runs through the wooded Den of Kildrummy, has no real village, though it includes the two hamlets of Nether Kildrummy and Milltown. The mansion of Kildrummy House is now a hotel, standing among delightful rock and climbing gardens. Across the ravine is ruined Kildrummy Castle, now in the care of the Scottish Development Department. Once a castle of the first importance when it was the seat of the earldom of Mar, it was the scene of the betrayal of Bruce's brother, Nigel. The twin drum towers of the gatehouse were the work of England's Edward I, who in 1306 managed to get into the castle thanks to the treachery of an English blacksmith. Sheltering under the hospitality of Bruce's sister, who had married Gartnait, Earl of Mar, there were, apart from Nigel Bruce, the queen, the king's sisters and the Princess Marjory. The castle was again defended by Bruce's sister at the time of the Balliol usurpation. The Wolf of Badenoch seized Mar's heiress and forcibly married her here to gain the earldom for himself. James III's favourite, the architect Cochrane, was given the earldom of Kildrummy, an elevation that no doubt helped accelerate his death, for he was hanged from the parapet of Lauder Bridge by the jealous nobles. Kildrummy was in Elphinstone hands until 1626, when the Erskine Earls of Mar came once more to own it. It fell to Cromwell's troops, and was later a centre for Mar's rising of 1715, after the failure of which it was finally dismantled.

The parish church of Kildrummy lies on a side road, further along the A97, and dates from 1805. On the top of a hillock stand the ruins of the old church, below which was the burial vault of the Mars and the grave of Christian Bruce.

Lumsden is a planned village, built in 1840 by a laird of Clova. It has a grassy village square, and a former Free Church of 1843 that now serves as the parish church, its abandoned predecessor two miles away doubtless being thought too far away from the village itself.

Rhynie, a large village on the Moor of Rhynie, is something of an archaeologists' paradise, with Pictish relics in profusion all around it. Its village green is railed in, and contains four standing stones, apparently all that survives of a stone circle.

From the little Deeside town of Banchory, to Alford on the A980, the road bends through the holiday village of Torphins, developed to its present size from a mere hamlet with the coming of the railway to Deeside in 1859. The section of the main street with the Learney Arms Hotel and the Learney Hall, a large granite building put up by Colonel Francis Innes in 1898 to commemorate his parents' sixtieth wedding anniversary, is less attractive than the higher tree-sheltered part of the village standing on the knoll from the Gaelic for which—*tor-fionn*, 'a light-coloured knowe'— the place presumably took its name. There is a church curiously reminiscent of South German architecture dating from 1875 and, on a road beyond, Learney House, seventeenth century in origin but added to and altered after a fire in 1837. One twentieth-century laird was Sir Thomas Innes of Learney, a redoubtable Lord Lyon King of Arms.

Lumphanan, said to mean 'bare little village', is memorable mainly because, at a spot now marked by Macbeth's Cairn, Macduff is reputed to have killed Macbeth on 15 August 1057. More certainly, Edward I stopped off at the peel tower here in 1296 to receive the submission of Sir John Malevill. In James VI's time it possessed a parish minister famed for the dubious skill of being able to bring considerable numbers of witches to trial and certain execution.

The parish church, near the peel tower and to the south of the village, dates from 1762, and though still small, was actually enlarged in 1851. Lumphanan, sloping to the sunny south, is a pleasant village, though part-girdled with some modern housing none too inspired.

Alford, on the A944, is a long and large village, shaped around a road junction. There is an ugly monument to the Farquharsons. At Alford West, the parish church dates from 1804, though it was enlarged in 1826. The Aberdeenshire poet Charles Murray (1864–1941), well-loved in the north-east for such Scots pieces as "The Whistle" and "Gin I was God", lived for a time in a house called Murrayfield, and a public park now commemorates him.

Though Whitehouse, between Alford and Aberdeen scarcely merits a second glance, Dunecht, outside the policies of the great Victorian home built by the Cowdray family, has interesting rows of prosperous-looking estate cottages. Between this road and the A96, down the B993, lies Monymusk, which gives its name to a great estate and a little village. The village is a planned one, neatly built round a green. Monymusk House and Church are both of considerable interest. The church had been preceded by a Culdee settlement before Gilchrist, Earl of Mar, built a priory in 1170 and enforced the Augustinian order. The priory chapel became the parish church at the Reformation, an imposing building with a huge sandstone tower. During restoration in 1932, two Norman arches were revealed. The church has several treasures, including some fine seventeenth- and eighteenth-century silver, two Pictish stones preserved at the foot of the nave arch, and some locally wrought but tasteful modern ironwork.

The most famous local treasure of all, the Monymusk Reliquary, dating from the seventh century and ornamented with precious stones, was believed to contain one of St Columba's bones. It came from the ancient priory, only a few traces of which still remain. Kept for generations in Monymusk House, the reliquary is now in the permanent safe keeping of the Museum of Antiquities in Edinburgh.

The house, a little north-east of the village, stands on the banks of the Don. It is a substantial cluster, gathered round a keep built by William Forbes in 1587. Sir Francis Grant, raised to the Lords as Lord Cullen, bought Monymusk from Sir William Forbes in 1712. It is said that Sir Francis's son, Sir Alexander, planted more trees than anyone else in eighteenth-century Britain. Lord Cullen's second son, William Grant, later Lord Justice Clerk Prestongrange, features in Stevenson's *Catriona*. The Grants still own Monymusk.

A mile to the north-west, sixteenth-century Pitfichie Castle was allowed to fall into near ruin when it came to the Forbes. Before that, one of its owners was General Hurry, the Civil War soldier who fought both for and against Montrose.

The great house of Auchleven, on the B992, Lickleyhead Castle, is a fortalice put up in 1629 for the Leith family. Insch, further north along the road, is a large granite-built village, well provided with shops. Its parish church tower dates from 1883. Its predecessor is now simply an ivy-clad gable. Near the village are the remains of the castles of Dunnideer and the restored Harthill, now in American hands.

On the A96, from Aberdeen to Huntly, Blackburn lies just about half way to the stone-built burgh of Kintore. Blackburn was originally called Broadford of Glasgo, and grew up to service a distillery in 1821. The distillery, however, failed, leaving behind it housing that has matured into a pleasing village. The parish church, in a remote and hilly position a mile and a half to the north, dates from 1801, but it has a bell cast in 1615.

Pitcaple, beyond the town of Inverurie (from where the weaver poet William Thom came) now has a fairly large modern development, a quarry, and the lived-in castle of the Lumsdens, who acquired it by marriage to a Leslie heiress in 1757. James IV and Mary, Queen of Scots are numbered among its visitors. She planted a thorn tree which survived her by about three hundred years. Charles II came here after landing from Holland in 1650. Montrose was brought captive to Pitcaple on his journey from Assynt to execution in Edinburgh.

The Bennachie mountain range is much in evidence hereabouts. Between Inverurie and Pitcaple the Battle of Harlaw took place in 1411. It put an end to even the remote possibility of Highland domination of the whole of Scotland, and was celebrated in verse by Lady Wardlaw.

There are few villages of any consequence as the road moves towards Keith, although Pitmachie and Old Rayne, on either side

of the River Urie, are typically rural hamlets. So, too, is Colpy.
Cairnie, half way between Huntly and Keith, was the birthplace
of the portrait painter William Aikman (1682–1731). Its church,
under the Bin Hill, has a large belfry and in the kirkyard the remains of an earlier edifice containing the Pitlurg Aisle, the burial
place of the Gordons of Pitlurg and Botary. The inscription on
the remains of a curious effigy at the rear of the arch records
that "Sir John Gordone of Pitlurge, Knycht, caust big this ile" in
1597.

Cairnie is, so to say, the starting point of the north-east bothy
ballad of "Drumdelgie". It captures the hard run of the farm
labourer's life, more vividly than the facts and figures of the
sociologist:

> There's a farmie up in Cairnie,
>   That's kennt baith far and wide,
> Tae rise i' the mornin' early
>   Upon sweet Deveronside.
>
> At five o' clock we quickly rise.
>   And hurry doon the stair,
> To get oor horses a' well corned,
>   Likewise to straught their hair . . .

After a hasty breakfast, "generally brose", the gaffer calls the men
to work.

> The mill goes on at sax o' clock,
>   To gie us a strait wark,
> And sax o' us we mak' to her
>   Or ye could wring oor sark. . . .
>
> When daylight it begins to dawn,
>   The sky begins to clear,
> The gaffer shouts "Hallo my lads,
>   You'll stay nae langer here.
>
> There's sax o' you'll gae to the plough,
>   And twa can ca the neeps,
> And the oxen they'll be after you,
>   Wi' stray raips roon their queets. . . ."

So the labourer was not sorry when the working day ended:

Sae fare ye weel, Drumdelgie,
  For I maun gang awa',
Sae fare ye weel, Drumdelgie
  Your weety weather and a'.

Fare ye weel, Drumdelgie,
  I bid you all adieu
I leave as I got ye—
  A damned unceevil crew.

Two miles to the north-east of Cairnie is the sheltered little village of Ruthven, its now vanished castle once the home of the Gordon chief Tam o' Ruthven.

Along the A920 from Aberdeen to the town of Turriff, the first sizable village is Newmachar, which owes its growth in part to the mental hospital at Kingseat. Elrick House, a Georgian mansion off the B979 Fintray road, came to the Burnett family in the middle of the seventeenth century, the wife of the first Burnett laird being the sister of the Scottish portrait painter George Jameson (c. 1588–1644). The landscaped gardens received and nurtured the famous Fassifern Rose, faithfully transported from Prince Charles Edward Stuart's villa in Rome. Cuttings have also been established at the royal garden of Balmoral.

Two miles north of Newmachar, Straloch House, built by John Ramsay of Barra in 1760, was the seat of Robert Gordon of Straloch (1580–1661), mapmaker, geographer and scientist, the first graduate of Marischal College and the founder of Aberdeen's Robert Gordon's College.

On the B999, the curiously named hamlet of Whiterashes leads to Udny, a pleasant sloping village that has a green, a granite parish church with a square tower built in 1821, and the gates of Udny Castle. The oldest part of the Udny keep dates from the fifteenth century, and there are sixteenth- and seventeenth-century additions. Extensive Victorian accretions were removed during a twentieth-century restoration, a model of its kind.

Though only a mile to the north-east, Pitmedden on the B9000, is more easily reached from the Ellon to Old Meldrum road. Apart from the orderly St Meddan's Terrace, this agricultural settlement is not particularly attractive, most people's reason for visiting it being nearby Pitmedden House's sunken Great Garden with sun-dials, horologes, fountains and flanking pavilions built by Sir Alex-ander Seton, Lord Pitmedden of Session, in 1675. It is now in the care of The National Trust for Scotland. A mile to the north-west is Tolquhon, a splendid ruined courtyard castle with a drum tower, once the home of the Prestons of Craigmillar and now in the care of the Scottish Development Department.

Tarves, on a small ridge, has spoiled its appearance by turning its village green into a tarmacadamed car park. Its most attractive end lies to the north. Its Melvin Hall is the gift of Andrew Car-negie. At the east of the village is the parish church, built in 1798 but altered in 1825. The Tolquhon Tomb, in the kirkyard, was part of the Tolquhon Aisle of the pre-Reformation church of St Englatius, a saint whom even the most saintly admit to being pure invention! Sir William Forbes, seventh laird of Tolquhon and a Renaissance-inspired man of taste, had this memorial built for himself in 1589.

Methlick stands mainly on one side of a road in a valley facing northwards across the Ythan valley. Its Gothic parish church and impressive clock-tower are of 1866 vintage, its roofless predeces-sor situated a little to the north and dedicated to St Devenick, still with its bell hanging dumb in its belfry. The Gordons, Earls of Aberdeen, are buried here. Their home, Haddo House, recently acquired by the Secretary of State for the nation, is a Palladian mansion built in 1732 by William Adam, one of the most impres-sive great houses in Scotland. The present Lady Aberdeen became famous for the use to which she and the late Lord Aberdeen put the wooden hall in the grounds, built by the seventh Earl and first Marquis (of the *We Twa* partnership). In 1948, she created from local talent the Haddo House Choral Society. It has since mounted a succession of first performances of major works, attract-ing some of the world's leading musicians to play for her locally-recruited singers. I recollect recording for the B.B.C. an interview with the aged Vaughan Williams, come to listen to his *Sea Sym-phony* and to conduct Parry's "Blest Pair of Sirens". Though an infinitely greater composer than Parry, 'V.W.' would only agree to talk in praise of his one-time master. On another occasion I found myself by chance interviewing Benjamin Britten for a television programme; the first time, if I recollect correctly, that he agreed to allow himself to be filmed for this purpose.

On the A947 from Old Meldrum, a neat little town, to Turriff is the picturesque village of Fyvie, celebrated in the north-east ballad "The Bonnie Lass o' Fyvie". It stands on rising ground set back from the River Ythan. Once it had a seminary in its priory of St Mary, headed by a mid-fourteenth-century Prior, Thomas Cranno, who believed that students, "if obstreperous . . . once out of sound of the secular world, should be soundly flogged". A cross, put up in 1868, marks the site of St Mary's. The church, put up in 1808, has a Dutch bell dated 1609, a castle pew and laird's loft and some early twentieth-century stained glass by the celebrated jewellery firm Tiffany of New York. Cranno's stone has been removed from the earlier church of St Peter, and is to the left of the chancel. Alexander Seton, Lord Fyvie, who died in 1603, is commemorated by a painted wooden panel. Four Pictish stones are built into the east gable. Among the gravestones are those of some of Byron's ancestors, the Gordons of Gight. Ruined Gight Castle lies further east, up the Ythan.

Fyvie Castle, a mile to the north, is an impressive and extensive L-shaped fortalice. Its double drum-tower dates from the seventeenth century, but the building contains nearly every possible enrichment of castellated architecture to be found in Scotland. Its royal visitors have included William the Lion and Alexander II, as well as the doubtless rather less welcome Edward I of England. Montrose had a near escape from Argyll's forces here in October 1644, at the 'Skirmish of Fyvie'. Cromwell garrisoned the castle. A royal seat until 1380, the future Robert III made it over to Sir John de Lindsay. From the Lindsays it passed through Prestons, Meldrums, Setons and Gordons to its present owners, the Forbes-Leiths.

A mile north-east of the castle is Mill of Tifty, the source of "Mill of Tifty's Ballad", whose prototype was Agnes Smith. She died in 1678.

That flat, rich agricultural corner of Scotland of which the fishing ports of Buckie, Fraserburgh and Peterhead roughly form a triangle, has a host of villages and hamlets too numerous to mention.

Longside, on the A950, has a steepled church dating from 1835, hard by its ruined predecessor in the churchyard where the tombstones include one erected in the nineteenth century to Jamie Fleming, 'the Laird of Udny's fool', who died in 1778. Another commemorates John Skinner, the author of the song "Tullochgorum" and other Scots pieces, who died in 1807 at the age of eighty-six in the arms of his son, the Episcopalian Bishop Skinner. The Skinner cottage at Linshart still survives. The Episcopal church of St John's, built in 1853, holds a museum-case containing Skinner's Prayer-book of 1637, pewter communion vessels and some silver spoons.

From the Cairngall quarry, to the east of Longside, came the stone used for much of the Bell Rock Lighthouse, the Houses of Parliament and the old Covent Garden Market.

Mintlaw, a nineteenth-century village has lost its village green to provide a well-landscaped traffic roundabout.

Old Deer, in the valley of the South Ugie Water, is probably the most attractive of the villages in Buchan. Its main street has two imposing churches which dominate the scene. The parish church dates from 1788, though it was restored almost a century later. Its ruined predecessor has a Norman arch. The Episcopal church of St Dunstan's includes among its stained-glass windows one in honour of Viscount Claverhouse, 'Bonnie Dundee', and another in honour of St Margaret, Malcolm Canmore's wife. Fetterangus, two miles to the west, is a rather unattractive eighteenth-century village with its own green; proof, in a small way, that age does not always mellow into charm where the built environment is concerned.

New Deer is a hilly linear village, formerly called Auchreddie, and developed into its present shape because it lies at the crossroads of A948 and A981. Its Gothic church and clock-tower were put up in 1865. A mile to the west, at Bruce Hill, Edward Bruce, the King's brother, is said to have camped before defeating the Comyns at Aikey Brae in 1308. Maud, between the two Deers, is situated in pleasant countryside and has the scanty ruins of the former Keith stronghold of Clackriach Castle, but is not itself of great interest.

The small town, or large village, of Strichen, on the A981, was formerly called Mormond. Mormond Hill has a White Horse cut on its western slopes and a stag on its south-eastern, the former the work of an eccentric laird, a certain Captain Fraser, who founded the hamlet of New Leeds in an unsuccessful attempt to rival the industrial achievement of the older Yorkshire city of the name. Strichen was laid out in 1764 by his son, who became Lord Strichen of Session, also with the aim of promoting industry. Though nowadays not unattractive, the ambitions of its founder were not quite realized. Today, the former Free Kirk, at the north end of the village, has replaced as parish church the original late eighteenth-century building, a mile to the south, and now abandoned. The former Strichen House, the work of Gilpin, was built by the ironmasters, the Bairds of Gartsherrie. They bought the estate from the Frasers, who moved south on heiring the Lovat peerage. The house is now a shell.

New Pitsligo, at the junction of A90 and A852, was founded by Sir William Forbes of Pitsligo, a village a mile long. Lace is still manufactured here. Once there were granite quarries associated with the place.

New Aberdour is an L-shaped village founded by William Gordon of Aberdour in 1798 in impressive surroundings. Its plain kirk dates from 1818. The old ruined kirk, on a shelf above the Deer Burn, a mile to the north, is attractive and, according to the *Book of Deer*, was founded by Columba himself, who came here from Iona with his pupil Drostam.

Back once more to the coast road, the A92, and proceeding north from Stonehaven, there are several attractive villages on the coast by-passed by an overland journey. Muchalls—originally Stra'nathro, the present name being adopted early in 1900—has a fine castle, dating from the early seventeenth century, though built round an earlier nucleus. Originally Fraser property, the Burnetts of Leys were its owners by 1619 and it is still privately owned. The village, properly Seatown of Muchalls, incorporates the fishing village and the harbour of Stra'nathro. It is to some extent a commuting village for people working in Aberdeen, and many of the former fishers' cottages have been well restored. The fine seaboard has remarkable cliff scenery. Newtonhill, Skateraw and Cammachmore, the latter a little inland, are also well restored, mostly as commuter villages. Findon, a little to the north, was the original home of the yellow smoked haddock, still a delectable dish. Cove Bay, a cliff top fishing community, has an attractive harbour, and, unlike many other such villages, a good road linking village and harbour. It is now a popular holiday resort.

North of Aberdeen, the first village of distinction is Newburgh, a large settlement on the mouth of the Ythan. It enjoys a remarkable position on the estuary of that river, a haunt of wild fowl, and accordingly much favoured by naturalists. Unfortunately, this attractive village is marred by an abandoned warehouse and mill at its northern end. The church of the Holy Rood was built as a chapel-of-ease in 1882, successor to a pre-Reformation chapel founded by Comyn, Earl of Buchan, in the time of Alexander III and known as the Red Chapel of Buchan. The village has a typically Scottish vaulted ice-house for the storage of fish, Newburgh having once been a salmon fishing port.

Across the estuary, beyond the Sands of Forvie, lies Collieston, a delightful Buchan fishing haven and holiday resort. It stands on a cliff top, overlooking a rocky bay called St Catherine's Dub, and provides good harbourage. One of its restored fishermen's houses, the Captain's Cabin, is constructed out of a ship's deckhouse.

North of the village is Kirkton of Slains, marked by a severe looking parish church of 1800, surrounded by the burial place of the Hays of Erroll, whose castle of Old Slains lies a little to the north. Nearby is all that is left of Old Slains Castle, high above the raging sea. Near it the late Countess of Erroll, hereditary High Constable of Scotland and thirty-first Chief of Clan Hay, built herself a modern house on the site of her ancestors' courtyard.

The coastal resort of Cruden Bay is of minor literary interest, in that 'Bram' Stoker—brother of Sir William Thornley Stoker, the elderly friend of Florence Drysdale, who late in life became Thomas Hardy's second wife—is said to have had the idea for his story of Dracula there. The great palace of the Erroll family, where

Johnson found himself unable to sleep during a night in 1773 because of the noise of the waves, nevertheless seemed to him the noblest he had even seen. Sold to the shipowner Sir John Ellerman in 1916, it was dismantled nine years later. Two miles to the north are the famous Bullers of Buchan. Hatton, three miles to the west, is a large village with a flourishing biscuit factory.

Boddam, the fishing village on a headland by Buchan Ness—almost, but not quite, an island, even though a bridge is crossed to reach it—is within sight of one of Robert Stevenson's lighthouses, built in 1827. The village is gathered close about the large harbour, and is still in use as a fishing port. The dignified harled church dates from 1865. All that is left of Boddam Castle is now a single gable, but once it was a fortalice of the Keiths of Ludguharn, dating from the fifteenth century. Just short of Peterhead is the village of Burnhaven, closer to Peterhead Prison than the town after which it is named. It is not a particularly attractive place.

North of Peterhead, the village of St Fergus lies a little back from the A92. At the east end is its parish church, dating from 1763 though largely renewed in 1869. The manse dates from 1766. St Fergus has become the landfall point for natural gas from the North Sea. Further up the A952 is the village of Crimond, not a very attractive place with a parish church dating from 1812. The belfry clock bears the threatening message: "The hour is coming". It was after the village of Crimond that one of the best-known Scottish psalm tunes was named. A mile to the west is Logie, associated with the Jacobite ballad "Logie o' Buchan".

St Combs, on the coast, like Inverallochy, has no harbour. St Combs is now largely a commuting village for Fraserburgh, though Inverallochy and its neighbouring fishing village of Cairnbulg across the now covered Allochy Burn still have a few boats drawn up on sandy beaches. They are about the best examples of the north-east fishing village, with their close-set rows of fisher cottages end-on to the sea, allowing just enough room between them to enable fishing-boats to be drawn up for repair during the winter. The ancestors of the Norwegian composer Edvard Grieg lived just outside Cairnbulg, and lie buried now in Rathan cemetery. Beyond Kinnaird Head, Sandhaven is another one-time fishing village, not unattractive but now mostly occupied by dwellers other than fishers. Rosehearty, on the other hand, a place of marked character, has a large harbour still in use, although without the thriving bustle of former days. The Dower House at Pitsligo, which dates from 1573 and has an eighteenth-century addition is, unfortunately, now completely roofless, as is nearby Pittulie Castle. The regularly patterned streets of Rosehearty make it amount almost to a town, although the cottages at the west end, gable ends to the streets, bespeak its fisherfolk origin.

Retracing our steps to take in by-passed ground, further along the coast into Banffshire, the village of Crovie, a conservation area, shelters in the lee of Troup Head. It is possibly one of the most unusually attractive of all Scotland's fishing villages to tourists, although it must have been a depressing place to have had one's home. Nowadays, its houses, one gable facing the sea, the other frontage a bank of the ravine beneath which the village clusters precariously, are mostly holiday homes. Founded in the eighteenth century it is curiously divided by a burn flowing into Gamrie Bay.

The road from this village to Pennan, on the coast, is spectacular and varied. Pennan itself is an extremely picturesque village, its long row of cottages sheltering, as it were, under the cliffs for protection. Many of its former fishermen's cottages are now holiday homes, though a little inshore fishing is still carried on from the harbour. There are romantically named caves and rock features near this village, which is well worth visiting.

Past the busy fishing port of Macduff, and the well-conserved burgh of Banff, we come to another fishing village, Whitehills. With its grouping of cottage gable ends, its rock-bound harbour and the ancillary industries of fishing surrounding it, it still gives an impression of modest prosperity. Portsoy, its steep streets leading down to its now deserted harbour, has had many of its eighteenth-century houses splendidly restored as council housing in recent years, particularly round the harbour, and is in every way a most attractive place. From Portsoy came the green marble used to provide two chimney-pieces for Louis XIV's Versailles. Souvenirs are now locally made out of Portsoy marble.

Beyond the small town of Cullen, Portknockie and Findochty, both conservation areas, echo the pattern of coastal fishing villages from which much of the original purpose has departed. Buckie and Macduff are now the ports from which most of the local fishing boats work.

One nearby inland place deserves a visit, the outstanding conservation area of Fordyce. This little red sandstone village, with its winding lanes, its miniature sixteenth-century castle built by Thomas Menzies, an Aberdeen burgess, and its ruined church dedicated to St Tarquin, attracted considerable attention during European Architectural Heritage Year 1975. The present church dates from 1804.

The hinterland of Banffshire, famous for its distilleries, soon becomes increasingly Highland in character. There is a similar division between the coastal strips of Moray and Nairn and the Highland hills that back them. The fishing industry along this coastline considerably expanded in the earlier years of the nineteenth century when Highlanders were compulsorily settled in these parts at the time of the Clearances; a sad event in Scottish history movingly told in Neil M. Gunn's magnificently sweeping novel, *The Silver Darlings*.

At the mouth of the Spey, Garmouth was the landing-place of Charles II in 1650. Under duress (as he later saw things) here he signed the Solemn League and Covenant. Kingston-on-Spey was a considerable shipbuilding centre during the nineteenth century, but is now once again a quiet village.

Fochabers, perhaps now almost a town, is an excellent example of a large planned eighteenth-century village, built to resettle the population of the old village felt to be too close to Gordon Castle for the lordly tastes of the times. Bellie, the old name of the parish, survives attached to the eighteenth-century church in the centre of the place.

Branderburgh and Seafield, though interesting in themselves, are now really part of the town of Lossiemouth, given its wider fame through having been the birthplace of one-time Prime Minister Ramsay MacDonald. Westward along the coast is Burghead, almost a town in itself, but a place worth visiting because of the so-called Roman well, which in fact is a Pictish bath-chamber cut out of solid underground rock. The name of the place derives from the borg or fortress of Earl Sigurd of Orkney, who established it in the year 889 near the site of an earlier vitrified Pictish fort. The harbour is used by the Outward Bound School, and there is a coastguard station from which, on a fine day, there is an uncommonly wide-ranging view. Annually on 12 January, the 'Burning of the Clavie' takes place. A blazing tar barrel is rolled down Dorrie Hill, an interesting ritualistic survival from Pictish times. A B.B.C. transmitting mast was put up in 1936 on Clarkly Hill, to the east of which is the small village of Cummingstown.

Findhorn village, a conservation area, is a breezily exposed little place with a good heritage of eighteenth-century houses. It is the third village to occupy the site. Its two predecessors proved to have been even more vulnerable to the wind and the waves, because one disappeared under the shifting Culbin Sands, whose treacherous movement has now been largely stabilized by tree-planting, while another suffered through a change of course of the Findhorn River. Some salmon fishing still goes on, although the harbour, built in 1840, is now used mainly by pleasure craft. The Crown Inn, built in 1739, Kimberley, dated 1777, the Quay Lodge of 1775 and the nineteenth-century James Milne Institute are among the more interesting individual buildings, though the real charm of the place is its grouping. The one-time Free Kirk, now the Church of Scotland, dates from 1843. Inland from Findhorn on the main Aberdeen–Inverness road, Alves has a fine 1769 church, now sadly fallen into disuse. Auldearn has a well-preserved doocot—all that survives of its now disappeared great house—owned by The National Trust for Scotland where the plans are set out for the scene of what many consider to have been Montrose's most brilliant battle in 1645.

Only the foundations of the abbey of Kinloss, a Cistercian settlement of 1159, survive. Indeed, the name is now commonly associated with R.A.F. Kinloss, who for many years have operated a Mountain Rescue Unit and manned sea searching aircraft from the airfield outside the village. Nearby Duffus Castle, of royal origin, went to Sir Edward Bruce of Clackmannan after the Reformation.

He became Lord Bruce of Kinloss, father of the first Earl of Elgin. Duffus was sold to the Brodies, who in turn disposed of much of the masonry to Cromwell for use in his fort at Inverness.

Westwards, Inverness becomes increasingly the magnet of local activity and attraction. There are pleasant villages in Nairnshire—for instance, the outstanding conservation area of Cawdor, built to serve the well-preserved Cawdor Castle, associated by Shakespeare with Macbeth—but their ambience is unmistakably Highland. It therefore only remains to make a foray into the Black Isle, then move round the Cromarty Firth and up the eastern coasts of Sutherland and Caithness to John o' Groats, beyond which lie Orkney and Shetland, whose people would not only repudiate the notion that they were Lowland Scots, but the very suggestion they were Scots at all!

8

The Far North

THE Black Isle, or Ardmeanach (which in Gaelic means the 'height between') as it is really called, is not an island at all, but a long peninsula with a hilly spine, the Millbuie range. It has coastlines on the Moray Firth, to the south, and the Cromarty Firth, to the north. Not only is the Black Isle not an island, but it also is in no real sense black. The usual explanation for this extraordinary misnomer is the fact that in winter, when snow often covers the higher Highland hills, the low-lying Black Isle remains free of snow, and thus seems black by comparison with the white heights.

Kessock, named after the Celtic St Kessock and divided into north and south by the sea-passage linking the Beauly Firth with the Moray Firth, is Highland by associations and scenic outlook. South Kessock is a suburb of Inverness. North Kessock, over the ferry, now almost merges with the fishing village of Charlestown. Its pier was built by Sir William Fettes (1750–1836), the founder of Fettes College in Edinburgh and one-time owner of the estate of Easter Kessock. The village stretches along the seafront, enjoying dramatic Highland sea loch views. It was here that the greatest novelist the Highlands has produced, Neil M. Gunn (1891–1974) spent his last years.

Munlochy, at the head of Munlochy Bay, really a sea loch that at low tide displays a vast stretch of coppery sand, looks towards the Sutors of Cromarty, those great heads of land that mark both sides of the loch's entrance. Munlochy has a wishing well, where wishers present themselves on the first Sunday in May. On the north coast, on Lady Hill, there stood the castle of Ormond, now only a grassy mound but once the home of the famous Regent Moray. After a spell in Douglas hands, the Crown annexed it. James III made his second son Duke of Ross, Marquis of Ormond and Earl of Edirdale, a curious word deriving from Eradour, another ancient name for the Black Isle. Nearby is another wishing well, that of Craigoch, where wishes are reputed to be fulfilled more readily if accompanied by a gift from the wisher.

Avoch, pronounced 'Och', still has an active fishing community. It is at the heart of Mackenzie country. The estate of Rosehaugh was once the seat of Sir George Mackenzie (1639–91), author of the first Scottish novel, *Aretina*, a famous Lord Advocate, founder of the Advocates' Library in Edinburgh, but to the Covenanters simply 'Bloody Mackenzie'. They could hardly be expected to acknowledge that his prosecution of them was simply the carrying out of the law of the land. Avoch sits in a hollow dominated by two churches both raised on hilly ground. The Free Church, on the Gallow Hill, is as bleak and unforgiving as the doctrines its upholders have historically professed. The parish church, dating from 1670 but enlarged both in the eighteenth and nineteenth centuries, stands across the burn on Braehead, and has a bell that once belonged to Fortrose Cathedral. Cromwell removed it, along with much of the stonework from the cathedral, when he was plundering local cultural monuments to build his fort at Inverness. However, while being transported on a ship across the Firth it was washed overboard and only dredged up in the mid-nineteenth century by a fisherman from Avoch. In the kirkyard is the grave of Sir Alexander Mackenzie of Avoch (1764–1840), discoverer of the Northwest Territories in Canada, after whom the Mackenzie River is named. So strong is the Mackenzie influence that the streets of the village are also named after members of the Mackenzie family. There is a tradition that many of the Avoch fisherfolk are descendants of survivors from a wrecked galleon of the Spanish Armada. Generations of overlaying Scottish blood are not likely to have left many traces of Spanish temperament among them. Some of their cottages turn their gable-ends to the street, as in the fishing villages of Moray and Buchan. There have been three buildings on or near the site of Avoch House. The home of 'Bloody Mackenzie' gave place to a Victorian mansion. It has in turn been replaced by a modern house.

Fortrose and Rosemarkie, twin small towns or large villages, however you choose to look at them, straddle Chanonry Point. Since 1592 they have together formed the royal burgh of Fortrose. They have a strange tradition linking them with the Borders. Michael Scott, the famous wizard, is reputed to have instructed the fairy host to build a cathedral at Elgin and a Chanonry Church at Fortrose. It may well be asked why this unusual architectural patron should have interested himself at all in furthering the cause of a rival branch of the supernatural. Tradition is silent on that point. Unfortunately, it is equally silent about the fairy error that subsequently occurred. Medieval fairies and modern workmen seem to have in common a lack of interest in the task upon which they are engaged. The fairies built the two buildings on the sites meant for each other. The wizard, though doubtless annoyed, evidently possessed some taste, for he decided to let both buildings stand, so to say, where they stood: more than can be said for Knox's Reformers or Cromwell's Roundheads when they later came, respectively, to Elgin and Fortrose. Of Fortrose Chanonry, only the south aisle, the chapter house, and the sacristy now survive, their reddish stones dignifying the green square around which some of the old church houses still stand. Notable is the Dean's House, and the Georgian Town House.

In the High Street, near the corner of Academy Street, is the shaft of the old mercat cross. The Academy of 1791 has been extensively rebuilt in our own time. The Episcopal church of St Andrew has some good stained glass. Inside the Town Hall, itself a former church, a collection of portraits of the Seaforth family from Brahan Castle has been brought together. It includes one of Kenneth Mackenzie, the famous 'Brahan Seer', some of whose prophecies the long arm of coincidence has conveniently brought to pass.

Rosemarkie—the *Rose* prefix, common hereabouts, derives not from the flower, but from the Gaelic *ros*, a promontory—nestles under high sandstone cliffs, on a raised beach. St Moluag and St Boniface both established cells here, though the present church dates only from 1821. It does, however, possess a communion cup of 1640 and a pewter baptismal bowl of 1742, as well as some silver in safe keeping elsewhere. Outside the church is a Pictish slab, elaborately decorated, but showing signs of wear. Beneath the church is a vault, discovered in 1735. It is supposed to contain the remains of St Boniface. It is known to contain those of the Regent, Sir Andrew Moray.

By the harbour is another of those traditional vaulted ice-houses, surviving from the days when Rosemarkie was a local centre for the salmon-netting industry.

After Haddington, in East Lothian, Cromarty is possibly the most complete old Scots burgh to come down to us in the twentieth century comparatively unaltered. Like Haddington, Cromarty has been largely by-passed by history, though by-passed so distantly that its active life has seriously ebbed with the steady twentieth-century centralization of day-to-day activities. The sea once rose to a higher level than it does now, and washed part of the older vernacular Cromarty away. Even so, its eighteenth- and nineteenth-century houses, designed with the good taste of local tradition and adding up to a satisfyingly mature grouping, do wear an air of serious decay. Unless some positive means of rehabilitating Cromarty is found soon, its outstanding conservation area status will be of little avail. Unfortunately, at the time of writing, petty local rivalries have hindered recent attempts at organizing the corporate restitution of the burgh.

A church and graveyard once stood below the Fishertown, the position indicated by the Kirk Stanes. To the Vikings, Cromarty was *Sykkerssand*, while to that voluble eccentric, perhaps its most distinguished son, Sir Thomas Urquhart of Cromarty (c. 1605–60), *Portus Salutis*.

Today, it is doubtful if many more people read the books of the geologist-author Hugh Miller (1802–56) than those of Urquhart. Miller's cottage is now owned by The National Trust for Scotland, and, whitewashed and thatched, attracts a surprising number of readers of *My Schools and Schoolmasters* and *The Old Red Sandstone.* Miller was reputed once to have seen the ghost of his ancestor, John Fiddes, who built the cottage in 1711. Handyside Ritchie's life-size statue of the stone mason, geologist and author stands on a forty feet high column. The old castle of the Urquharts, six storeys high, battlemented and with a stone roof, was demolished in 1772 to make way for the first Cromarty House, put up by the Rosses, who succeeded the Urquharts in the eighteenth century. However, a sixteenth-century fireplace was taken from the old and built into the new house.

Again, it retains the sense of a community that must once have been a satisfying social entity, thriving against both the elements and the challenge of the outside world. Of individual buildings, the eighteenth-century Sheriff Court House is the most interesting. It has a clock tower and ogee-capped cupola, and a bell cast in 1571. The mercat cross outside is unusual in that it still has its cross finial. It bears the double date 1578 and 1770. The church is one of the oldest to survive in the Highlands, dating from 1700. It has good eighteenth-century fittings inside.

The Fishertown, a cluster of typical cottages, has a school below which is yet another ice-house, used when Cromarty was an active fishing port. It is odd to think that from the harbour, now given over mainly to pleasure craft, £25,000 worth of goods were shipped to London in 1807, twenty-two years after its quay had been constructed. By 1880, that quay had to be extended. At the end of the nineteenth century, Cromarty had become the principal centre of the fishery district between Findhorn and Helmsdale Loch. In 1894, apparently a good year, 2,258 barrels of white herring, besides cod, ling and hake, were taken by 286 boats, employing 998 fishermen and boys. One of its eighteenth-century lairds, George Ross, established a brewery to discourage the fishermen and others from drinking whisky. It has also lost both its hemp and cloth factory and its ropeworks. Today, really alive only at the height of the tourist season, it awaits much-merited restoration, a shell from Scotland's past across the water from the twentieth-century profile created by the oil industry.

There are no villages of outstanding interest on the southern shore of the Cromarty Firth. Cononbridge, which takes its name from the River Conon on the right bank of which it is built, came into being when the river was first bridged to carry the road from Beauly to Dingwall in 1809, one of the many road and harbour works carried out by Thomas Telford in the Highlands and north-eastern fringe of Scotland. It is now virtually joined to Maryburgh. Conon House, a Mackenzie home built in 1758, had the youthful Hugh Miller working on it as a mason when it was being constructed.

The northern shores of the Cromarty Firth have increasingly been given over to the oil industry. Evanton, east of Dingwall, has a curious former Free Church school at the end of the principal cross-street of the village. It has been acquired by a local society for conversion to a history museum. South of the village, by the Firth, is the atmospheric ruin of Kiltearn Church, formerly the parish church. Milton, a conservation area, has had considerable restoration work carried out on its privately owned houses. Both have experienced an increase in population and of course the passage of oil-industry related traffic. There may be those who regret the more drastic scenic effect upon such places as Alness and Nigg. However, the great Highland cry of protest for centuries has been that no work-centre with job opportunities on a large scale existed above the Highland line. The kind of prosperity that has come to the Cromarty Firth, even if it has not perhaps quite matched the original expectations, and, due to bad contracting, in one respect at least is a heavy drain on the taxpayer, should not therefore be a subject for aesthetic complaint, though there are grounds for anxiety in that few if any of its present industries are likely to survive the comparatively short-term oil era.

Balintore, on the Tarbat–Nigg peninsula, forming the outer stretch of the Moray Firth, is a fishing hamlet linked with Hilton of Cadboll. The most celebrated of all Pictish cross-slabs, the Cadboll Stone, depicting vigorous hunting scenes, is in the National Museum of Antiquities. It was discovered on a mound a little to the north of the village. Only two or three vaults survive of Cadboll Castle, next to the shores of the Dornoch Firth. The inland village of Fearn, grouped round its village green and war memorial, has a ruined abbey, used as a parish church until 1742, when the roof fell in, killing forty-four Protestant worshippers. It would not be particularly noteworthy except that in one of its whitewashed cottages Peter Fraser, New Zealand's Prime Minister from 1940–49, was born.

The conservation area village of Portmahomack—the name derives from *Port na Colmac*, 'the harbour of Colmac'—sits on a sandy bay by the entrance to the Dornoch Firth. Its harbour was one of many in this part of the world rebuilt and extended by Thomas Telford in the early nineteenth century. Some unhappy modern infill houses rather spoil the waterfront line of the village, but it is still an attractive place. A dignified warehouse of former days at the head of the pier has crow-stepped gables and dates from the seventeenth century. The Castle Hotel is an early nineteenth-century hostelry, behind which, on a bank closing the village to the east, is the site of St Colmac's Chapel. St Colmac's well, a little to the south, has fallen into disrepair.

Past the charming royal burgh of Tain, now a little town, lies Edderton, on Cambuscurrie Bay. It witnessed a curious reversal of the usual state of affairs at the time of the Disruption. The old parish church of 1743 was taken over by the Disrupters, the minority Establishment having to build their own new kirk, which they did nearer the village, though with an optimism on the matter of the size of congregations to be accommodated that must surely have been belied even in the 1840s.

Through the linear roadside village of Ardgay and on past Bonar Bridge Station, the A9 crosses the Kyle of Sutherland. Like Ross and Cromarty, Sutherland stretches right across Scotland, and possesses such a wealth of glorious scenery that the comparative bleakness of its east coast strip is of little enough matter. Dornoch, Golspie and Brora, through which the A9 winds, are little towns like Helmsdale, which lies at the mouth of the river of the same name. Outwardly they are Lowland places, but the temperament of their inhabitants is predominantly Highland.

The main road to Thurso turns up Strath Kildonan and makes its eventual way up to Halkirk, where the roads to Thurso and Wick divide. Up the coastal road, through the Ord of Caithness— a place often blocked by snow in a bad winter—the road hugs the sea. Berriedale and Borgue are not particularly remarkable, though Dunbeath Castle, a little south of the village of Dunbeath, had its moment of glory. Standing on a sea cliff, and now part of a nineteenth-century house, the ancient baronial fortalice was captured in 1650 by General Hurry for the Marquis of Montrose. Dunbeath was the birthplace of the most distinguished novelist to come out of the Highlands, Neil M. Gunn (1891–1974). The beautiful Strath through which flows the Water of Dunbeath provides the locale for much of his novel *Highland River*, and the beach at Dunbeath is described at the opening of *Morning Tide*. Latheran, linked to Janetstown, still has a quaint fishing harbour which, along with the harbour head cottages and houses, is protected by conservation area status.

Lybster was once the centre of the fishing industry on this stretch of the Caithness coast, putting to sea nearly one hundred and fifty boats at the end of the nineteenth century. Staxigoe shares with Berriedale a name of Norse origin—Berriedale derives from the Norse word *Berudalr*—and with Latheran conservation area status for its harbour. Its two storehouses date from the days when the Earls of Caithness accepted grain in lieu of rent.

From the earliest times of human habitation in Scotland, there were settlements along this northern coast. Pictish slabs are to be found throughout the north-east fringe of Scotland. At Keiss, explorations uncovered Stone Age burial cysts and implements more than a century ago. There are many later castles in various stages of ruin, most of them picked clean even of legend by the northerly winds. The days of Norse domination, and the days of the Sinclair Earls who succeeded them, were times when violence was a commonplace occurrence. William Sutherland, otherwise known as 'Big William, the Son of Hector', was compelled to embark on a raid on Orkney with one of the Earls of Caithness. Sutherland, having a premonition that he might not return alive, lay down on the green above Berriedale Inn, and had a grave of appropriate size cut out of the ground. His premonition proved correct. His burial place became known as the 'Long Grave', since it measured 9 feet 5 inches in length.

Watten with its loch near which, at Halsary and Moss of Wester

Watten, the remains of Pictish houses or weems have been found, has the typical grey Caithness weathered look. To the north-west of the church, at Stonehouse, a standing stone is reputedly the burial place of Skuli, an Orkney Jarl. Backlass, two miles west by south of the village, was the home at the end of the eighteenth century of David Marshall, regarded as the Rob Roy of the north.

Reay, by the head of Sandside Bay, stands on what was once apparently a burgh of regality, rediscovered as the result of a water spout in 1751. The mercat cross is supposed to have come from the older burgh, where Donald Mackay, the first Lord Reay, was knighted by James VI in 1616.

It is not for its villages that one visits Caithness. The country-side is flat and windswept. In the days when the stone flags used for making pavements in many Scottish cities were still being quarried in Caithness, farmers employed them standing on their sides end-to-end as a wind-breaking substitute for both wall and fence. With the virtual demise of the quarrying industry, this unique feature of the Caithness landscape is now, unfortunately, dis-appearing in favour of wire fencing. Apart from its excellent fish-ing and its bracing expanses of summer light—though also of windswept winter darkness—Caithness is known to the wider world because of the spectacular atomic station at Dounreay—an astonishing sight both from the sea and from the surrounding countryside—Elizabeth, the Queen Mother's home of Castle of Mey, and John o' Groat's house, which generations of children have suggested, rather selfishly, to Rainy Rattlestones as a more appropriate target for his precipitations than wherever they hap-pened then to be.

From the headlands by the hotel, the modern traveller looks over the Pentland Firth towards Stroma and Orkney. By the time he has reached these northern shores, he will certainly have realized that with his circumnavigation of the great northern firths, the 'feel' of the countryside of Easter Ross and Sutherland has become unmistakably Highland, however flat the topography. Similarly, Caithness is imbued with the starker qualities of sea and land, peopled by the fringes of those same long shadows of Norse myth that still provide so striking a background to the lives of twentieth-century Orcadians.

By the simple, if somewhat artificial, process of considering only the level of the terrain, this survey has contrived to link the lusher villages of Berwickshire, at one end of Scotland, with their starker Caithness counterparts at the other. In every respect other than that of a more or less common flatness, these extreme edges of Scotland share very few characteristics. No matter. The encompassing variety of Scotland is one of its greatest charms.

Index

Index

M